It's another Quality Book from CGP

*This book has been carefully written for
children working towards a Level 6.*

It matches the Attainment Targets perfectly.

*There's lots of stuff to learn if you're taking the Level 6 Extension Test.
Happily this CGP book explains all the important information
as clearly and simply as possible.*

What CGP is all about

*Our sole aim here at CGP is to produce the highest quality books
— carefully written, immaculately presented and
dangerously close to being funny.*

*Then we work our socks off to get them out to you
— at the cheapest possible prices.*

Contents

Section Four — Measuring

Section Five — Handling Data

Section Six — Using and Applying Mathematics

Published by CGP

Editors:
Paul Jordin, Sharon Keeley-Holden, Alison Palin, Caley Simpson, Dawn Wright.

ISBN: 978 1 84762 442 0

With thanks to Alison Griffin, Simon Little and Lorraine Young for the proofreading.

Groovy website: www.cgpbooks.co.uk

With thanks to Laura Jakubowski for the copyright research.
Thumb illustration used throughout the book © iStockphoto.com.

Printed by Elanders Ltd, Newcastle upon Tyne.
Jolly bits of clipart from CorelDRAW®

Based on the classic CGP style created by Richard Parsons.

About the Book

This Book has All the Tricky Topics for Level 6

You've got a good chance of getting a <u>Level 6</u> if you can do <u>all the maths</u> in this book.

There are a couple of pages on each topic.

One page <u>explains</u> the maths.

The other page has <u>worked examples</u>.

These show you how to answer questions.

This book covers all the <u>Attainment Targets</u> for Level 6. They say what maths children working at Level 6 can usually do.

There are Practice Questions for Each Section

At the end of each section are <u>practice questions</u>.

You can see what you know and what you don't know.

There's a <u>matching Level 6 Question Book</u>.

It's got questions on all the topics.

It also has some practice tests too.

I love to practise.
I love to practise.

There are Learning Objectives on All Pages

Learning Objectives say <u>what you need to know</u>.

Use the <u>tick circles</u> to show how well you understand the maths.

Use a pencil. You can <u>tick other circles</u> as you get better.

I can win gold
at the Olympics.

Tick here if you can do some
of the Learning Objective.

If you're struggling,
tick here.

Tick this circle if you can do the
Learning Objective really well.

Learning Objective:

"I can add and subtract fractions
by using a common denominator."

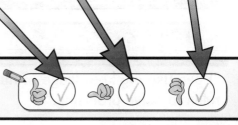

Numbers

Remember These Types of Number

FACTORS of a number are whole numbers that <u>divide exactly into</u> that number.

   EXAMPLE: The factors of 18 are 1, 2, 3, 6, 9 and 18.

A COMMON FACTOR of two numbers is any number that's a <u>factor of both numbers</u>.

MULTIPLES of a number are just its <u>times table</u>.

   EXAMPLE: The multiples of 7 are 7, 14, 21, 28, 35, ...

A COMMON MULTIPLE of two numbers is any
number that's a <u>multiple of both numbers</u>.

A PRIME NUMBER has <u>exactly two</u> factors — itself and 1.

   EXAMPLES: 7 is a prime number: its only factors are 1 and 7.
                 8 is not a prime: its factors are 1, 2, 4 and 8.

> 1 is <u>not prime</u> because
> it only has <u>1 factor</u>.

A SQUARE NUMBER is a whole number <u>multiplied by itself</u>.

   EXAMPLES: $25 = 5 \times 5 = 5^2 =$ "5 squared"
                  $36 = 6 \times 6 = 6^2 =$ "6 squared"

> A little ^{2} means
> 'squared'.

Rules for Negative Numbers

When you <u>multiply</u> or <u>divide</u> positive (+) and negative (−) numbers,
there are <u>rules</u> to tell you if the <u>answer</u> is <u>positive or negative</u>.

> **To × or ÷ two numbers:**
> If the signs are <u>the same</u>, the answer is <u>positive</u>.
> If the signs are <u>different</u>, the answer is <u>negative</u>.

> There's an <u>invisible '+' sign</u>
> before any positive number.

EXAMPLES:
   $-2 \times 3 = -6$ The signs are different, so you get −6, not +6
   $12 \div -3 = -4$ The signs are different, so you get −4, not +4
   $-6 \times -8 = +48$ The signs are the same, so you get +48, not −48

There are rules for <u>adding</u> and <u>subtracting</u> positive and negative numbers too.

> **To + or − two numbers:**
> Two of the <u>same sign</u> next to each other means +.
> Two <u>different signs</u> next to each other means −.

EXAMPLES:
$5 - -6 = 5 + 6 = +11$
$3 + -4 = 3 - 4 = -1$

Learning Objective:

"I can use my knowledge of number
rules to solve problems."

Numbers

Question 1

Joel is thinking of a number. His number is greater than 6 and less than 24.
It is a multiple of 6 and it is a factor of 24. What number is Joel thinking of?

1 Start by listing the first few multiples of 6.

2 We want a number greater than 6 and less than 24. That leaves 12 or 18.

3 See which is a factor of 24 — if it's a factor it'll divide exactly into 24.

Multiples of 6:
6, 12, 18, 24, 30, ...

Greater than 6, but less than 24:
6, 12, 18, 24, 30, ...

$24 \div 12 = 2$ — so 12 is a factor of 24
$24 \div 18...$ — doesn't divide exactly, so 18 isn't a factor of 24

So Joel's number is 12.

Question 2

Preeti says "The square of a negative number is always positive."
Is she correct? Explain your answer.

1 Use what you know about square numbers and negative numbers to work out if Preeti's statement is true.

2 Make sure you explain each step clearly.

A square number is a number multiplied by itself.

So the square of a negative number is a negative number times a negative number.

When you multiply a negative by a negative, the answer is always positive.

So the square of a negative number is always positive. So Preeti is correct.

Plenty of facts — make sure you can use them...

For explainy-type questions, you might need to use different number rules together to solve problems. Make sure you understand the different types of number on these pages.

Big and Small Number Scales

Work Out the Size of the Steps

Some number lines show really big or really small numbers.
You should be able to read both types by working out what each small step is worth.

EXAMPLE: What number is the arrow pointing to on this number line?

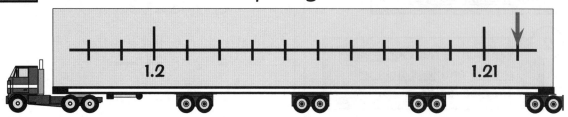

1) The difference between the numbered marks is 1.21 – 1.2 = 0.01
2) Work out how many steps there are between these numbers.

> Remember to count the number of steps, not the number of small marks in between.

3) Here there are 10 steps from 1.2 to 1.21, so each one is worth 0.01 ÷ 10 = 0.001.
4) So the arrow is pointing to 1.21 + 0.001 = 1.211.

You Might Need to Estimate Points on the Line

The scale used on some number lines makes it hard to find exact points.
In that case, you might just have to make a good estimate.
It often helps to add some extra marks to the number line.

EXAMPLE: Draw an arrow on the number line pointing to –241 000.

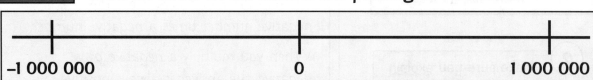

1) Split the left-hand (less than zero) side of the number line into four equal steps of 250 000.

2) –241 000 is a little bit nearer to 0 than –250 000, so put the arrow just to the right of the –250 000 mark.

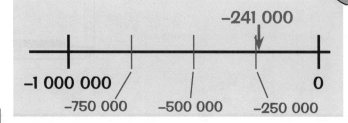

Learning Objective:

"I can use and understand number lines showing very large or very small numbers."

Big and Small Number Scales

Question 1

Part of a number line is shown below. Mark with an arrow the position of 0.58.

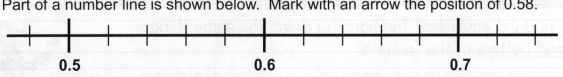

0.5   0.6   0.7

1   Find the <u>difference</u> between each numbered mark.

2   There are <u>5 small steps</u> from one numbered mark to the next, so <u>divide by 5</u> to find the size of each small step.

3   Count on from 0.5 in <u>steps of 0.02</u> until you get to 0.58.

Difference between each numbered mark is:
$0.6 - 0.5 = 0.1$

Each small step is worth $0.1 \div 5$:
$10 \div 5 = 2$, so $0.1 \div 5 = 0.02$

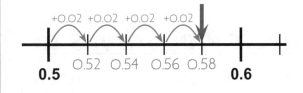

Question 2

Here is part of a number line. Estimate the value that the arrow is pointing to.

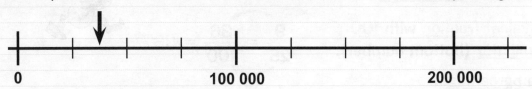

0   100 000   200 000

1   Work out what the <u>small steps</u> are worth.

2   The arrow's pointing <u>about halfway</u> between 25 000 and 50 000.

3   Count on <u>half a step</u> from 25 000. Half a step is $25\,000 \div 2 = 12\,500$.

Each small step is worth
$100\,000 \div 4 = 25\,000$

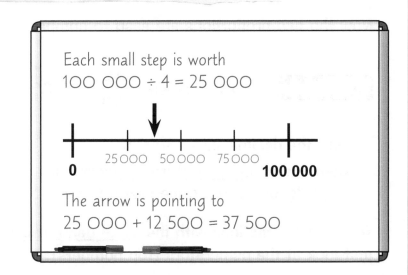

The arrow is pointing to
$25\,000 + 12\,500 = 37\,500$

It's all about those in-between marks...

It helps with number line questions if you're good at dividing — including dividing decimals. If you struggle with dividing, now's a good time to practise — it'll be a big help.

Fractions, Decimals and Percentages

Find Missing Numbers in Equivalent Fractions

Remember, you get <u>equivalent fractions</u> by doing the <u>same thing</u> to the <u>top and bottom</u> of the fraction.

EXAMPLE: What number should go in the box? $\dfrac{5}{6} = \dfrac{\square}{72}$

1) Work out what you do to get <u>from 6 to 72</u> on the bottom:

$$6 \underline{\times 12} = 72$$

2) Do the same to the top:

$$\overset{\times 12}{\underset{\times 12}{\frac{5}{6} = \frac{\boxed{60}}{72}}}$$

Convert Proportions to Compare Them

To compare fractions, decimals and percentages, convert them all to the <u>same type</u>. It's usually (but not always) easiest to change everything to percentages.

EXAMPLE: Which is greater, 42% or $\dfrac{9}{25}$?

Turn the <u>fraction</u> into a <u>percentage</u>:

1) Find an <u>equivalent fraction</u> with <u>100</u> as the <u>denominator</u> (bottom number).

2) Convert to a <u>percentage</u>.

$$\overset{\times 4}{\underset{\times 4}{\frac{9}{25} = \frac{36}{100}}} = 36\%$$

Now the two proportions are easy to compare: $42\% > 36\%$, so $42\% > \dfrac{9}{25}$

EXAMPLE: Which is greater, $\dfrac{13}{20}$ or 0.6?

1) Turn the decimal into a <u>fraction</u>.
2) Then find an <u>equivalent fraction</u> with the <u>same denominator</u> as the first fraction.

$$0.6 = \frac{6}{10} \overset{\times 2}{\underset{\times 2}{=}} \frac{12}{20}$$

To <u>compare</u> fractions with the <u>same denominator</u>, just look at the <u>numerators</u> (top numbers):

$$\frac{13}{20} > \frac{12}{20}, \text{ so } \frac{13}{20} > 0.6$$

Learning Objective:

"I can convert between fractions, decimals and percentages to compare them."

Fractions, Decimals and Percentages

Question 1

Put these three amounts in order from smallest to largest: 27%, 0.245, $\frac{63}{250}$

1 Convert the <u>decimal</u> to a <u>percentage</u> by multiplying by 100.

2 Find an <u>equivalent fraction</u> that converts easily to a <u>decimal</u>...

3 ...then convert to a <u>percentage</u>.

4 Remember to use the <u>original amounts</u> in the final answer.

$$0.245 \times 100 = 24.5\%$$

$$\frac{63}{250} \xrightarrow{\times 4} = \frac{252}{1000} = 0.252$$

$$0.252 \times 100 = 25.2\%$$

$$24.5\% < 25.2\% < 27\%$$

So in order, the amounts are

$$0.245, \frac{63}{250}, 27\%$$

Question 2

Find the number that should replace the question mark. $16\% = \frac{12}{?}$

1 Write the <u>percentage</u> as a <u>fraction</u> by putting it over 100.

2 16 and 100 both divide by 4, so you can <u>simplify</u> the fraction.

3 Work out what you need to <u>multiply</u> by on the <u>top</u> of the fraction, then <u>do the same</u> to the <u>bottom</u>.

$$16\% = \frac{16}{100} \xrightarrow{\div 4} = \frac{4}{25}$$

$$\frac{4}{25} = \frac{12}{?}$$

$$4 \times 3 = 12, \text{ so } \frac{4}{25} \xrightarrow{\times 3} = \frac{12}{75}$$

Percentages are always easy to compare...

If in doubt, convert all the numbers you want to compare to percentages. Then you won't need to worry about things like the number of decimal places or common denominators.

SECTION ONE — UNDERSTANDING NUMBER

Adding and Subtracting Fractions

Make Sure the Denominators are the Same

You can only add or subtract fractions with the <u>same denominator</u>.
That means you often have to find a <u>common denominator</u> for your fractions first.
Then you add or subtract the <u>numerators only</u>.

EXAMPLE: What is $\dfrac{1}{2} + \dfrac{1}{3} - \dfrac{1}{4}$?

First find <u>equivalent fractions</u> with the same denominator for each.

2, 3 and 4 are all factors of 12, so use 12 as a common denominator.

$$\overset{\times 6}{\dfrac{1}{2} = \dfrac{6}{12}} \qquad \overset{\times 4}{\dfrac{1}{3} = \dfrac{4}{12}} \qquad \overset{\times 3}{\dfrac{1}{4} = \dfrac{3}{12}}$$

Now add and subtract the <u>numerators</u> to get the answer:

$$\dfrac{1}{2} + \dfrac{1}{3} - \dfrac{1}{4} = \dfrac{6}{12} + \dfrac{4}{12} - \dfrac{3}{12} = \dfrac{6 + 4 - 3}{12} = \dfrac{7}{12}$$

You Can Add and Subtract Mixed Numbers

Turn <u>mixed numbers</u> into <u>improper fractions</u> before adding or subtracting them.

EXAMPLE: What is $5\dfrac{1}{6} - 2\dfrac{5}{6}$?

Convert the mixed numbers to <u>improper fractions</u>:

$$5\dfrac{1}{6} = 5 \times \dfrac{6}{6} + \dfrac{1}{6} = \dfrac{30}{6} + \dfrac{1}{6} = \dfrac{31}{6}$$

$$2\dfrac{5}{6} = 2 \times \dfrac{6}{6} + \dfrac{5}{6} = \dfrac{12}{6} + \dfrac{5}{6} = \dfrac{17}{6}$$

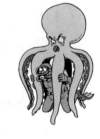

Turn the answer back into a mixed number if you can.

So $5\dfrac{1}{6} - 2\dfrac{5}{6} = \dfrac{31}{6} - \dfrac{17}{6} = \dfrac{31 - 17}{6}$

These fractions already have a common denominator.

$$= \dfrac{14}{6} = \dfrac{12}{6} + \dfrac{2}{6} = 2\dfrac{1}{3}$$

Learning Objective:

"I can add and subtract fractions by using a common denominator."

Adding and Subtracting Fractions

Question 1

Complete this calculation:

$$5\frac{1}{4} + 7\frac{3}{5} = ?$$

Write your answer as a mixed number.

1 Change the mixed numbers into improper fractions.

2 Find a common denominator for the fractions.

3 Add the numerators of the fractions.

4 Turn the answer back into a mixed number.

$$5\frac{1}{4} = 5 \times \frac{4}{4} + \frac{1}{4} = \frac{20}{4} + \frac{1}{4} = \frac{21}{4}$$

$$7\frac{3}{5} = 7 \times \frac{5}{5} + \frac{3}{5} = \frac{35}{5} + \frac{3}{5} = \frac{38}{5}$$

$$\frac{21}{4} \xrightarrow{\times 5} = \frac{105}{20} \qquad \frac{38}{5} \xrightarrow{\times 4} = \frac{152}{20}$$

$$5\frac{1}{4} + 7\frac{3}{5} = \frac{105}{20} + \frac{152}{20}$$

$$= \frac{257}{20}$$

$$= \frac{240}{20} + \frac{17}{20} = 12\frac{17}{20}$$

Question 2

Percy has a jar of elastic bands. Half of the elastic bands are red, two-sevenths of them are green and the rest are blue. What fraction of the elastic bands in Percy's jar are blue?

1 Write the problem in numbers first.

2 Find the fraction of elastic bands that are not blue by adding the fractions of red and green.

3 Find the blue fraction by taking the non-blue fraction away from 1.

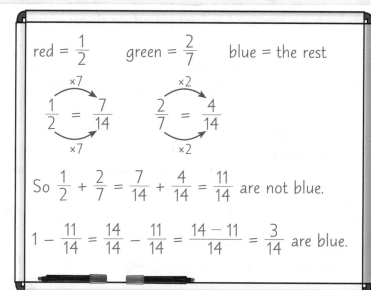

$$\text{red} = \frac{1}{2} \qquad \text{green} = \frac{2}{7} \qquad \text{blue} = \text{the rest}$$

$$\frac{1}{2} \xrightarrow{\times 7} = \frac{7}{14} \qquad \frac{2}{7} \xrightarrow{\times 2} = \frac{4}{14}$$

So $\frac{1}{2} + \frac{2}{7} = \frac{7}{14} + \frac{4}{14} = \frac{11}{14}$ are not blue.

$1 - \frac{11}{14} = \frac{14}{14} - \frac{11}{14} = \frac{14 - 11}{14} = \frac{3}{14}$ are blue.

Mixed numbers: wot, sneve, fountree...

You must remember — to add or subtract fractions, make sure they've got the same denominator, then only add or subtract the numerators. It just won't work otherwise.

Fractions and Percentages Problems

Fractions or Percentages of Amounts

To find a <u>fraction</u> of an amount, you <u>divide</u> by the <u>denominator</u> and <u>multiply</u> by the <u>numerator</u>. For <u>percentages</u>, convert to a fraction first, then do the same.

EXAMPLE: Find 40% of 350.

40% is the same as $\dfrac{40}{100} = \dfrac{4}{10}$ ($\div 10$)

'of' means '$\times$'

$\dfrac{4}{10}$ of 350 $= \dfrac{4}{10} \times 350 = (350 \div 10) \times 4$

$= 35 \times 4 = 140$

You need to know how to write one number <u>as a fraction</u> or <u>a percentage</u> of another number too.

EXAMPLE: There are 15 girls and 10 boys in Mario's class. What percentage of the class are girls?

1) First write the <u>total amount</u> as the <u>denominator</u> of the fraction.

2) Then write the <u>number of girls</u> as the <u>numerator</u>.

3) Convert the fraction into a <u>percentage</u>.

$15 + 10 = 25 \longrightarrow \dfrac{}{25}$

$\dfrac{15}{25} = \dfrac{60}{100} = 60\%$ ($\times 4$)

Finding Percentage Change

When an amount is increased or decreased, you can work out the <u>percentage change</u>.

> The percentage change is the <u>actual change</u> as a percentage of the <u>original amount</u>.

In a sale, you might see '<u>10% discount</u>'. 10% is the percentage change.

EXAMPLE: CGP Cinemas have just reduced the size of a small serving of popcorn from 240 g to 180 g. By what percentage have they reduced the size?

1) First work out the <u>size of the change</u>: 240 g – 180 g = 60 g

2) Write this as a percentage of the <u>original amount</u> (240):

$\dfrac{60}{240} = \dfrac{1}{4} = \dfrac{25}{100} = 25\%$ ($\div 60$ $\times 25$)

Learning Objective:

"I can give one number as a fraction or percentage of another, and solve percentage problems."

Fractions and Percentages Problems

Question 1

A pet shop has 4000 fish in stock. 15% of the fish are tetras, $\frac{3}{10}$ are guppies and the rest are goldfish.

How many goldfish does the shop have?

1 Work out <u>how many</u> tetras and guppies the shop has.

number of guppies $= \frac{3}{10}$ of 4000

$\quad\quad = (4000 \div 10) \times 3$
$\quad\quad = 400 \times 3$
$\quad\quad = 1200$

number of tetras $= 15\%$ of 4000

$\quad\quad = \frac{15}{100} \times 4000$

$\quad\quad = (4000 \div 100) \times 15$
$\quad\quad = 40 \times 15$
$\quad\quad = 600$

2 <u>Take away</u> those two amounts from the total to find the number of goldfish.

So number of goldfish
$= 4000 - 1200 - 600 = 2200$

Question 2

Kei buys a fishing rod for £80. He sells it for £96. What is Kei's percentage profit?

1 First work out the <u>size of the profit</u>. Remember that the profit is the amount he <u>makes</u> (the selling price – the original cost).

Amount of profit $= £96 - £80$
$\quad\quad\quad\quad\quad\quad = £16$
Original amount $= £80$
Percentage profit

2 Now write this profit as a percentage of the <u>original value</u>.

$$= \frac{£16}{£80} = \frac{1}{5} = \frac{20}{100} = 20\%$$

$\div 16 \quad \times 20$

$\div 16 \quad \times 20$

For percentage change, divide by the original amount

Watch out for percentage change questions — they don't always use the word 'change' in the question. It might say something like 'profit', 'loss', 'increase' or 'decrease' instead.

Ratios and Proportion

Find One Part in Proportion Questions...

EXAMPLE: 7 pineapples cost £6.30. How much will 4 pineapples cost?

> <u>Divide the price by 7</u> to find how much <u>FOR ONE PINEAPPLE</u>, then <u>multiply by 4</u> to find how much <u>FOR 4 PINEAPPLES</u>.

So...   £6.30 ÷ 7 = 0.9 = <u>90p</u>   (for 1 pineapple)
          90p × 4 = <u>£3.60</u>   (for 4 pineapples)

...and in Ratio Questions

EXAMPLE: Divide £600 in the ratio 7:5.

First, add together the numbers in the <u>ratio</u> to find <u>how many parts</u> there are in total: 7 + 5 = <u>12 parts</u>

Then:
> <u>Divide the £600 by 12</u> to find how much it is for <u>ONE PART</u> then <u>multiply by 7</u> to find how much <u>7 PARTS ARE</u> and <u>multiply by 5</u> to find how much <u>5 PARTS ARE</u>.

So... £600 ÷ 12 = <u>£50</u> (for 1 part)
          £50 × 7 = <u>£350</u> (for 7 parts)
and £50 × 5 = <u>£250</u> (for 5 parts)

So £600 split in the ratio 7:5 is   <u>£350 : £250</u>

> You can check the answer by adding the amounts:
> £350 + £250 = £600

Reducing Ratios to their Simplest Form

You <u>simplify ratios</u> just like you simplify <u>fractions</u>.

EXAMPLE: Write the ratio 15:18 in its simplest form.

1) Both numbers have a <u>factor</u> of 3, so <u>divide them by 3</u>.

2) We can't reduce the ratio 5:6 any further.
   So the simplest form of 15:18 is <u>5:6</u>.

$$= {}^{\div 3}\!\!\diagdown \begin{matrix} 15 : 18 \\ 5 : 6 \end{matrix}\!\!\diagdown{}^{\div 3}$$

Learning Objective:

"I can calculate using ratios."

Ratios and Proportion

Question 1

Divide £720 in the ratio 2:3:4.

1 Add up the number of <u>parts</u> in the ratio.

2 <u>Divide</u> to find the size of one part.

3 <u>Multiply</u> to find each share.

2 + 3 + 4 = 9 parts

£720 ÷ 9 = £80 per part

2 × £80 = £160
3 × £80 = £240
4 × £80 = £320

So £720 split in the ratio 2:3:4
is £160:£240:£320.

Question 2

Marina has a box of coloured counters. Two-fifths of the counters are green.
If Marina has 28 green counters, how many counters does she have in total?

1 You can do this as a <u>proportion</u> question.

2 <u>Divide by 2</u> to find the size of <u>one fifth</u> (one part).

3 The <u>whole</u> box is <u>five-fifths</u>. <u>Multiply</u> one fifth by 5 to get the total.

$$\frac{2}{5} = 28$$
÷2 ↘ ÷2
$$\frac{1}{5} = 14$$
×5 ↘ ×5
$$\frac{5}{5} = 70$$

So Marina has 70 counters.

Question 3

I have 18 orange frogs and 30 purple frogs.
Write the ratio of orange to purple frogs in its simplest form.

1 <u>Write out</u> the ratio and divide <u>both sides</u> by the <u>same number</u>.

2 Keep going until they <u>won't divide</u> any more.

orange : purple

= 18 : 30
÷2 ↘ ÷2
= 9 : 15
÷3 ↘ ÷3
= 3 : 5

Find the number of parts to divide a ratio...

Always think about what a question is asking. If it involves scaling up or down, or sharing in a ratio, finding the size of one part is often the best way to start.

SECTION ONE — UNDERSTANDING NUMBER

Practice Questions

1   Izzy is thinking of a number greater than 1.
It is a common factor of 28 and 42. It is not a prime number.

What number is Izzy thinking of?

2   Work out the numbers that should go in the boxes below.

a) $-10 \times 13 = \boxed{}$ b) $-54 \div \boxed{} = 6$ c) $\boxed{} \times -7 = -49$

3   For each of these number lines, write down the number the arrow is pointing to.

a)

6.2   6.25

b)

−500 000   0

4   Find the numbers that should go in the boxes below.

$$\frac{4}{\boxed{}} = \frac{12}{15} = \frac{\boxed{}}{60}$$

5   Rupinder and Saul sold tickets to the school play. At the start of the week, they each had the same number of tickets to sell. By the end of the week, Rupinder had sold $\frac{11}{15}$ of her tickets and Saul had sold 70% of his tickets.

Who sold the most tickets? Show how you know.

6   Mansour grows tulips in his garden.
One-seventh of the tulips are white. Four-ninths of the tulips are red.

What fraction of Mansour's tulips are either red or white?

SECTION ONE — UNDERSTANDING NUMBER

Practice Questions

7 Work out the answers to these calculations.
Give your answers as mixed numbers.

a) $3\frac{1}{2} + 2\frac{1}{5}$

b) $8\frac{1}{10} - 2\frac{3}{4}$

8 Gina has made 240 biscuits.
55% of the biscuits are orange flavoured. The rest are chocolate.

How many chocolate biscuits has Gina made?

9 Perry bought a bicycle for £75. He sold it for £57.

What was Perry's percentage loss?

10 Wesley is making identical superhero capes for all his family.
He has made 6 capes and used 7.2 m of fabric. He has another 8 capes to make.

How much more fabric will Wesley need?

11 Penny, Luc and Kelsey have found a treasure chest in the garden.
The chest contains 180 gold coins. Penny, Luc and Kelsey share
the coins between them in the ratio 10:5:3.

How many gold coins does each person get?

12 Erika has a collection of animal-shaped magnets.
She has 42 zebras and 14 lions.

What is the ratio of lions to zebras in Erika's collection?
Give your answer in its simplest form.

Sequences

You can Find a Rule for the Next Term...

Look at this number sequence: **2, 5, 8, 11, 14, 17, ...**

The rule is: <u>Add on 3</u> to get from one term to the next.

The trouble is, it would take you <u>ages</u> to find the <u>100th term</u> using this rule.

...Or you can Find the nth Term of a Sequence

The nth term is the aNythingeth term. So once you have a rule for finding it you can find the fourth, fifth, hundredth or thousandth term in the sequence. Wow.

EXAMPLE: Find the 20th term in the sequence 3, 7, 11, 15, 19, 23, ...

1) First find the <u>gap</u> between each number.
   This tells you the <u>times table 'family'</u> the sequence belongs to.

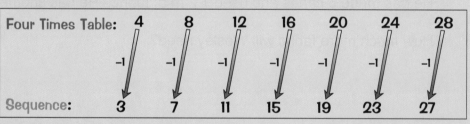

This sequence belongs to the <u>four times table family</u>.

2) <u>Compare</u> the sequence with the four times table.

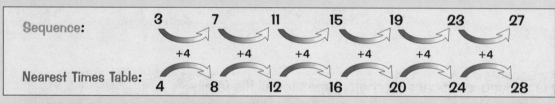

The sequence number is always <u>1 less than the number in the four times table</u>.

3) So the rule for the <u>nth term</u> is: "<u>multiply n by 4 and subtract 1</u>".
   You can write this as $4n - 1$.

The nth term in the four times table is <u>4n</u>. E.g. the 7th term is $4 \times 7 = 28$.

<u>Check</u> the rule using a term you know:
E.g. 3rd term: $(4 \times 3) - 1 = 11$. Yep. The 3rd term is 11.

4) The <u>20th term</u> will be: $(4 \times 20) - 1 = 80 - 1 = \underline{79}$

Learning Objective:

"I can describe a rule to find any term in a sequence."

Sequences

Question 1

Two terms of a sequence are given on the right.
The sequence is made by adding on the same number each time.
Find the first number of the sequence.

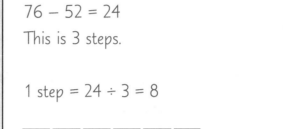

① **Work out the difference between the terms you're given and how many steps this is.**

② **Work out size of one step.**

③ **Fill in the sequence backwards until you get the first number.**

④ **Write the answer out clearly.**

$76 - 52 = 24$
This is 3 steps.

1 step = $24 \div 3 = 8$

| 36 | 44 | 52 | | | 76 |

−8 −8

The first term is 36.

Question 2

Boris is making a sequence of shapes using counters. Write a rule for the total number of counters in the nth term.

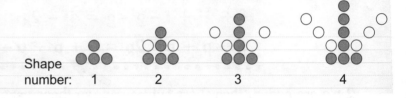

Shape number: 1 2 3 4

① **Find the number of counters in each shape. This is the sequence.**

② **Find the 'gap' between each term.**

③ **The gap tells you the times table family. Write out the start of this times table.**

④ **Compare the sequence terms to the times table.**

⑤ **Write the rule for the nth term.**

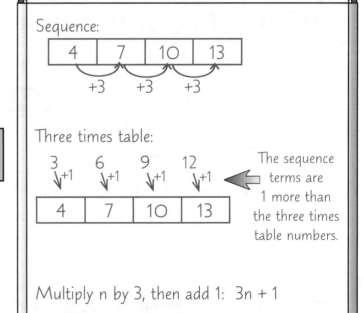

Sequence:

| 4 | 7 | 10 | 13 |

+3 +3 +3

Three times table:

3 6 9 12
+1 +1 +1 +1

| 4 | 7 | 10 | 13 |

The sequence terms are 1 more than the three times table numbers.

Multiply n by 3, then add 1: $3n + 1$

Finding the nth term means you can find any term...

For a sequence where you keep adding the same number, the nth term will always be 'something n, plus or minus a number'. The 'something' is always the times table number.

Expressions

Use Letters to Represent Unknown Numbers

You can use a <u>letter</u> to stand for a number that you don't know.

> If y is the unknown number then: $y + 3$ means you are <u>adding 3</u> to it.
>
> $y - 2$ means you are <u>subtracting 2</u> from it.
>
> $4y$ means you are <u>multiplying it by 4</u> ($4 \times y$).

<u>Expressions</u> contain letters and numbers. So '$y + 3$', '$y - 2$' and '$4y$' are expressions.

Expressions can also contain <u>letters multiplied together</u>:

> ab means $a \times b$
> a^2 means $a \times a$

Simplify by Collecting the Same Letters Together

You can only add or subtract the <u>same letter</u> together.

EXAMPLES:

$$b + b + b + b = 4 \times b = 4b$$
$$f + 2f + f - g - g = 4f - 2g$$
$$p + p + p - 2p = p + \cancel{p} + \cancel{p} - \cancel{p} - \cancel{p} = p$$

> You just write 'p' rather than '$1p$'.

2 p's are <u>added</u>, then 2 are <u>subtracted</u>, so these <u>cancel</u> each other out.

Multiply Everything in a Set of Brackets

If you've got something like $2(3 + a)$, remember this rule:

> The thing <u>outside</u> the brackets multiplies <u>each</u> bit <u>inside</u> the brackets.

EXAMPLE: Multiply out $3(y + 4)$

$$3(y + 4) = (3 \times y) + (3 \times 4) = 3y + 12$$

In any expression, <u>BODMAS</u> tells you the <u>order</u> you should do the calculations in:

So $(7 - 3) \times 5 + 2$
$= 4 \times 5 + 2 = 20 + 2 = 22$

<u>Brackets</u> first...   ...then <u>multiplication</u>...   ...then <u>addition</u>

B	Brackets
O	
D	Division
M	Multiplication
A	Addition
S	Subtraction

Learning Objective:

"I can simplify an expression and multiply brackets."

Expressions

Question 1

Simplify: a) 2 + c + 1 + 3c + 4   b) (2 × 3 × f × g) + (4 × g)

a) **1**   <u>Collect</u> the 'c's together and the numbers without letters together.

2   <u>Add up</u> the two groups separately.

b   Do the multiplications <u>before</u> the addition (<u>BODMAS</u>).

a) $\cancel{2} + \cancel{c} + \cancel{1} + \cancel{3}c + \cancel{4}$ = (2 + 1 + 4) + (c + 3c)

               = 7 + 4c

Cross out the bits as you go so you don't miss any.

b) (2 × 3 × f × g) + (4 × g) = 6fg + 4g

6fg and 4g can't be collected together because they don't contain exactly the same letters.

Question 2

Simplify: a) 3(k − 2) + 10   b) 4(y − 2) + 5(y + 3)

a) **1**   <u>Multiply</u> the **3** outside the brackets by <u>both bits</u> inside the brackets.

2   <u>Collect</u> any bits together that you can.

b) **1**   Multiply each set of brackets <u>separately</u>.

2   <u>Collect</u> any bits together that you can.

a) 3(k − 2) + 10 = (3 × k) + (3 × −2) + 10

               = 3k − 6 + 10

               = 3k + 4

You're adding 10 to −6 here so take care.

b) 4(y − 2) + 5(y + 3)

    = (4 × y) + (4 × −2) + (5 × y) + (5 × 3)

    = 4y − 8 + 5y + 15

    = 4y + 5y − 8 + 15

    = 9y + 7

Move the minus sign with the number it's in front of. It stays with the 8 here.

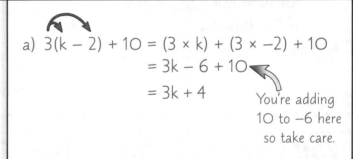

<u>You can only add terms with exactly the same letters...</u>

If you have a number multiplied by a letter, always write the number first, so 3b, not b3.
If there's more than one letter, it's best to put them alphabetically, so 3ab, not 3ba.

Formulas

A Formula is Used to Work Out an Amount

A formula tells you how to work out one quantity when you know a different quantity.
E.g. this formula is for working out how many legs a group of ants have altogether.

> L = 6a
> L = total number of legs
> a = number of ants

EXAMPLE: How many legs do 7 ants have altogether?

There are 7 ants, so <u>a = 7</u>.
<u>Substitute</u> 7 for a in the formula:

$L = 6a = 6 \times 7$

$L = 42$ legs altogether

Substitute is just a fancy word for swap.

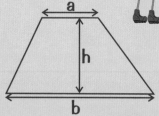

Here's a harder example:

EXAMPLE: The formula for the area of a trapezium
is $A = \frac{1}{2}(a + b) \times h$

Find the area of a trapezium where
a = 2 cm, b = 4 cm, h = 3 cm.

1 Write out the <u>formula</u>

2 Write it <u>again</u> underneath but with <u>numbers</u> in place of the letters.

3 Work it out in <u>stages</u>.

$A = \frac{1}{2}(a + b) \times h$

$A = \frac{1}{2}(2 + 4) \times 3$

$A = \frac{1}{2} \times 6 \times 3$

$A = 3 \times 3$

$A = 9$ cm²

Use <u>BODMAS</u> — so work out the <u>brackets</u> first.

Don't forget — the answer might need a <u>unit of measurement</u>.

You can Make Your Own Formula

This isn't as hard as it sounds. Just think about what you'd do if it were all numbers.

EXAMPLE: Hedgehog-flavoured crisps cost 35p a bag.
Write a formula for the total cost, T, of buying n bags.

<u>T</u> stands for <u>total cost</u>, <u>n</u> stands for the <u>number of bags</u>

In <u>words</u> the formula is: Total Cost = Number of bags × 35p

Putting the <u>letters</u> in: T = n × 35 or to <u>write it better</u>: T = 35n

Learning Objective:

"I can use a formula to work out a quantity."

Formulas

Question 1

It costs £13 to get into a fairground and £2 for each ride you go on.
The formula for the total cost, T, of going on r rides is: **T = 13 + 2r**

Work out the total cost of going on 7 rides.

1 — <u>Write out</u> the formula.

2 — Write it again underneath <u>substituting</u> r for the number of rides (7).

3 — Work it out in <u>stages</u>.
Use the <u>BODMAS</u> rules to tell you which order to do calculations in.

4 — Check if <u>units</u> are needed.

$T = 13 + 2r$
$T = 13 + (2 \times 7)$
$T = 13 + 14$
$T = 27$

Put brackets round this bit to remind you to do the multiplication before the addition.

It costs £27 to go on 7 rides.

It's got to be in pounds as the other values in the formula are in pounds.

Question 2

Temperatures can be given in degrees Celsius (C) or degrees Fahrenheit (F).
The formula for converting from degrees Fahrenheit to degrees Celsius is:

$$C = 5(F - 32) \div 9$$

Convert 50 degrees Fahrenheit to degrees Celsius.

1 — <u>Write out</u> the formula.

2 — Write it again underneath <u>substituting</u> F for the temperature in degrees Fahrenheit (50).

3 — Work it out in <u>stages</u>.
Use the <u>BODMAS</u> rules to tell you which order to do calculations in.

4 — Check if <u>units</u> are needed.

$C = 5(F - 32) \div 9$
$C = 5(50 - 32) \div 9$
$C = 5(18) \div 9$
$C = (5 \times 18) \div 9$
$C = 90 \div 9$
$C = 10$ degrees Celsius

Do the bit in brackets, then the multiplication and division.

Plonk the numbers in and calculate...

Formulas aren't half as scary as they look. Just remember to work out the calculations bit by bit, writing down each step. Oh, and use BODMAS to tell you which bit to do first.

Equations and Inequalities

Solve Equations to Find the Value of a Letter

Equations are things like 6y + 5 = 43, or 2 + 3c = 6c – 10.
Solving equations means finding out what each letter is worth. You do this
by getting the letter on one side of the "=" and the numbers on the other.

> Whatever you do to one side of an equation
> you have to do exactly the same to the other.

EXAMPLE: Find the value of b if 3b – 4 = 11

1 You want to end up with just the letter b on the
left-hand side. So get rid of the "– 4" by adding 4.
Remember to do the same to BOTH SIDES.

$$3b - 4 = 11$$
$$3b - 4 + 4 = 11 + 4$$
$$3b = 15$$

2 Now get rid of the 3 from the left-hand side by
dividing by 3. Don't forget to do it to BOTH SIDES.

$$3b \div 3 = 15 \div 3$$
$$b = 5$$

3 You've cracked it. But just to be on the safe side,
check your answer by trying it in the equation.

$$3b - 4 = 11$$
$$(3 \times 5) - 4 = 11$$
$$15 - 4 = 11$$

Yep, it works. → 11 = 11 ✓

Inequalities Show Which Side is the Biggest

13 < 3p < 25 means that 3p is greater than 13 but less than 25.
p could have more than one possible value and you might be asked to find them all.

EXAMPLE: 10 < 4k + 1 < 18. Find the possible values of k if k is a whole number.

Hmmm... let's try k = 2

$4k + 1 = (4 \times 2) + 1 = 9$
9 is smaller than 10, so k can't be 2.

> Remember, the bigger number goes at the big end of the inequality.

Try k = 3

$4k + 1 = (4 \times 3) + 1 = 13$
13 is greater than 10 but less than 18, so k could be 3.

Try k = 4

$4k + 1 = (4 \times 4) + 1 = 17$
17 is greater than 10 but less than 18, so k could be 4.

Try k = 5

$4k + 1 = (4 \times 5) + 1 = 21$
21 is greater than 18, so k can't be 5.

> Bigger values of k would make 4k + 1 more than 18 too.

So k could be 3 or 4.

Learning Objective:

"I can solve simple equations and inequalities."

Equations and Inequalities

Question 1

$7(a + 1) = 4a + 13$ Find the value of a.

1 The letter is on <u>both sides</u> of this equation. Don't worry — just get the <u>letters on one side</u> and the <u>numbers on the other</u> again.

2 Multiply out any <u>brackets</u> first.

3 Get rid of the '<u>+ 7</u>' from the left-hand side. It's added on, so <u>subtract</u> it off. As always, do the same to <u>BOTH SIDES</u>.

4 Get rid of the <u>4a</u> from the right-hand side, by <u>subtracting</u> it. Do the same to <u>BOTH SIDES</u>.

5 You're left with <u>3a = 6</u>. Get rid of the 3 from the left-hand side by <u>dividing BOTH SIDES by 3</u>.

$7(a + 1) = 4a + 13$

$7a + 7 = 4a + 13$

$7a + 7 - 7 = 4a + 13 - 7$

$7a = 4a + 6$

$7a - 4a = 4a + 6 - 4a$

$3a = 6$

$3a \div 3 = 6 \div 3$

$a = 2$

Check the answer by putting it into the equation:
$7(2 + 1) = (4 \times 2) + 13$
$7 \times 3 = 8 + 13$
$21 = 21$

Question 2

y is a positive whole number. What values can y have to make this statement true?

$$8 < y^2 - 3 < 25$$

1 Guess a value for y, e.g. <u>y = 3</u>. Try it in the <u>middle bit</u> of the statement to see if it makes the statement <u>true</u>.

2 y = 3 made the middle bit <u>too low</u>. Try a <u>bigger</u> number, e.g. <u>y = 4</u>.

3 4 might not be the <u>only</u> possible value for y, so try <u>y = 5</u>. Then try <u>y = 6</u>.

4 Higher numbers would make $y^2 - 3$ <u>greater</u> than 25, so you must have <u>found them all</u>.

5 <u>Write</u> the answer clearly.

$y^2 - 3 = 3^2 - 3 = 9 - 3 = 6$
6 isn't <u>greater than 8</u>, so y <u>can't</u> be 3.

$y^2 - 3 = 4^2 - 3 = 16 - 3 = 13$
13 is <u>greater than 8</u> and <u>less than 25</u>, so y <u>can be 4</u>. $8 < 13 < 25$

$y^2 - 3 = 5^2 - 3 = 25 - 3 = 22$
22 is <u>greater than 8</u> and <u>less than 25</u>, so y <u>can be 5</u>. $8 < 22 < 25$

$y^2 - 3 = 6^2 - 3 = 36 - 3 = 33$
33 <u>isn't less than 25</u>, so y <u>can't</u> be 6.

$y = 4$ or 5

Do the same to both sides of equations to keep them equal...

No matter what equation you're given to solve, just follow the same steps. It's like you're peeling the wrapping off the letter, layer by layer. Like pass the parcel with no music.

Trial and Improvement

Make your Guesses Better and Better

Sometimes algebra questions are too hard to answer by just doing one calculation. You have to use <u>trial and improvement</u>. You start by <u>guessing a value</u>, seeing what the result is, then picking <u>another value</u> to try.

EXAMPLE: x is a whole number. Which value of x makes $x^2 - 2x$ closest to 50?

① $7 \times 7 = 49$, which is close to 50, so try <u>x = 7</u>:

$$x^2 - 2x = (7 \times 7) - (2 \times 7)$$
$$= 49 - 14 = 35$$

② It's <u>less than 50</u>, so try a higher value and see if it makes the expression closer to 50: <u>x = 8</u>:

$$x^2 - 2x = (8 \times 8) - (2 \times 8)$$
$$= 64 - 16 = 48$$

③ This is <u>close</u>, but to make sure the next number isn't even closer try <u>x = 9</u>:

$$x^2 - 2x = (9 \times 9) - (2 \times 9)$$
$$= 81 - 18 = 63$$

x = 8 makes $x^2 - 2x$ closest to 50.

Finding Approximate Solutions

Sometimes a letter represents a <u>decimal value</u> rather than a whole number. You might have to decide <u>which whole number</u> it's <u>closest to</u>.

EXAMPLE: Solve $b^3 - b + 4 = 100$.
Give your answer to the nearest whole number.

$b^3 = b \times b \times b$

Pick any number to start with and make a table to record your guesses:

b	$b^3 - b + 4$	Too big or too small?
3	$(3 \times 3 \times 3) - 3 + 4 = 28$	Too small
10	$(10 \times 10 \times 10) - 10 + 4 = 994$	Too big
5	$(5 \times 5 \times 5) - 5 + 4 = 124$	Too big
4	$(4 \times 4 \times 4) - 4 + 4 = 64$	Too small
4.5	$(4.5 \times 4.5 \times 4.5) - 4.5 + 4 = 90.625$	Too small

Try a <u>bigger</u> number.

It's <u>smaller than 10</u> (but <u>more than 3</u>).

It's <u>between 4 and 5</u>. Try <u>4.5</u> to find which it's closest to.

It's between <u>4.5 and 5</u>. So it's nearer to <u>5</u> than 4.

b = 5 to the nearest whole number.

You might have to find a value to <u>1 decimal place</u> too — the second example on the next page shows this.

Trial and Improvement

Question 1

$x^2 + 7x - 2 = 58$ Find the value of x.

1 It's useful to make a <u>table</u> for your trials.

2 <u>Guess a number</u> (start with a fairly <u>small</u> one — it's easier to work out). <u>Substitute</u> this into the equation.

3 If the result is <u>too small</u>, try a <u>bigger value</u> of x. If it's <u>too big</u>, try a <u>smaller value</u> of x. Keep going until you find the <u>correct value</u>.

x	$x^2 + 7x - 2$	Too big or too small?
4	$(4 \times 4) + (7 \times 4) - 2$ $= 16 + 28 - 2 = 42$	Too small
6	$(6 \times 6) + (7 \times 6) - 2$ $= 36 + 42 - 2 = 76$	Too big
5	$(5 \times 5) + (7 \times 5) - 2$ $= 25 + 35 - 2 = 58$	Perfect

x = 5

Question 2

Meg knows that the area of her garden is 66 m² and that its width is 3 m shorter than its length. She is using the equation $x(x - 3) = 66$ to find the length of the garden, x, to 1 decimal place.

The table shows Meg's first three trials. Suggest the value of x which Meg should try next and give a reason for your answer.

x	x	x − 3

x	$x(x - 3)$	Too big or too small?
10	$10(10 - 3) = 70$	Too big
9	$9(9 - 3) = 54$	Too small
9.5	$9.5(9.5 - 3) = 61.75$	Too small

1 Decide which values x must lie <u>between</u>.

2 <u>Pick a number</u> between the two values and give the <u>reason</u> for this.

9.5 is too small and 10 is too big. So x must lie between them.

9.7 because I know x is bigger than 9.5 but less than 10.

9.6, 9.8, 9.9 or 9.75 are all correct answers too.

Keep on homing in on the number...

Here's the end of Meg's table from Question 2, above. x is between 9.75 and 9.8. So x = 9.8 to 1 d.p. Yay.

x	$x(x - 3)$	Too big or too small?
9.7	64.99	Too small
9.8	66.64	Too big
9.75	65.8125	Too small

Coordinates and Graphs

Work Out *x*-values and *y*-values to Draw a Graph

You can draw the <u>graph</u> of an <u>equation</u> by working out the <u>x-values</u> and
<u>y-values</u>, then <u>plotting</u> the <u>coordinates</u> and joining with a <u>straight line</u>.

> Coordinates tell you how many <u>across</u> and how
> many <u>up or down</u> from (0, 0) a point is.
>
> how many ⟶ **(x, y)** ⟵ how many
> across   up or down

> Remember — x <u>ALWAYS</u> goes
> <u>BEFORE</u> y To help you remember
> this, think 'x is <u>a-cross</u>' or 'go
> along the hall, <u>then</u> up the stairs'.

EXAMPLE: Plot the graph of y = 2x – 1

1) <u>Work out</u> some x-values and y-values by putting
<u>different numbers for x</u> into the equation:

x	2x – 1	y	(x, y)
1	(2 × 1) – 1 = 2 – 1	1	(1, 1)
2	(2 × 2) – 1 = 4 – 1	3	(2, 3)
3	(2 × 3) – 1 = 6 – 1	5	(3, 5)

Working out
<u>three points</u> is
usually enough
to be able to
plot the line.

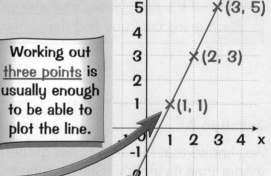

2) <u>Plot</u> the coordinates (1, 1), (2, 3) and
(3, 5) and join with a <u>straight line</u>.

Horizontal and Vertical Lines

Horizontal and vertical lines have really <u>simple</u> equations like x = –2 or y = 3.

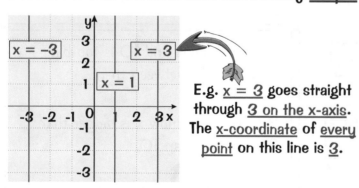

E.g. <u>x = 3</u> goes straight
through <u>3</u> on the x-axis.
The <u>x-coordinate</u> of <u>every</u>
<u>point</u> on this line is <u>3</u>.

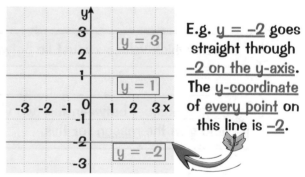

E.g. <u>y = –2</u> goes
straight through
<u>–2</u> on the y-axis.
The <u>y-coordinate</u>
of <u>every point</u> on
this line is <u>–2</u>.

The equation '<u>x = a number</u>' is
a <u>vertical line</u> that goes straight
through that number on the <u>x-axis</u>.

The equation '<u>y = a number</u>' is a
<u>horizontal line</u> that goes straight
through that number on the <u>y-axis</u>.

Learning Objective:

"I can use coordinates to plot graphs."

Coordinates and Graphs

Question 1

a) Complete the table below and plot the graph of the equation y = –2x + 3.

b) Does the point (32, –60) lie on the graph of y = –2x + 3?

a) **(1)** Complete the <u>table</u>.

Be REALLY careful with <u>negative</u> numbers. Some examples are shown.

(2) Use the <u>x and y values</u> from the table as <u>coordinates</u> (x, y). <u>Plot</u> them on the grid.

(3) Draw a <u>straight line</u> through the points with a <u>RULER</u>.

If the points <u>aren't</u> all in a straight line, you've done something <u>wrong</u>, so <u>check</u> your working.

b <u>Substitute</u> the <u>x-coordinate</u> into the graph's equation and see if it gives the <u>correct y-coordinate</u>.

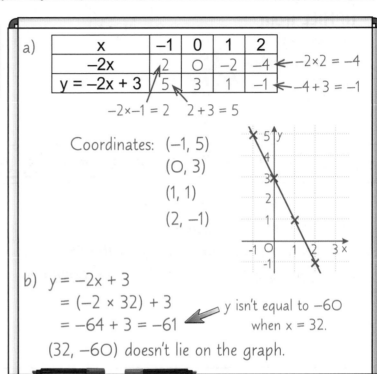

a)

x	–1	0	1	2
–2x	2	0	–2	–4	← –2×2 = –4
y = –2x + 3	5	3	1	–1	← –4 + 3 = –1

–2×–1 = 2   2 + 3 = 5

Coordinates: (–1, 5)
(0, 3)
(1, 1)
(2, –1)

b) y = –2x + 3
= (–2 × 32) + 3
= –64 + 3 = –61   ← y isn't equal to –60 when x = 32.

(32, –60) doesn't lie on the graph.

Question 2

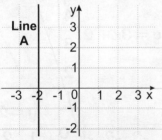

a) Write down the equation of Line A.

b) Line B is horizontal and crosses Line A at (–2, –1). Write down the equation of Line B.

a The line is <u>vertical</u>, so the equation must be <u>x = a number</u>. Look at where the line crosses the <u>x-axis</u> — this tells you what the number is.

b) **(1)** Mark on the <u>point</u> where the lines cross (–2, –1), and draw in the <u>horizontal Line B</u>.

(2) Write down the <u>equation</u> of Line B.

a) The vertical line goes through –2 on the x-axis, so the equation is x = –2.

b) Line B is horizontal and goes through –1 on the y-axis, so the equation must be y = –1.

Line B

(–2, –1)

Just plot the x and y values and join them with a line...

Remember — when you multiply a negative number by a positive number, the result is negative. When you multiply two negative numbers, you get a positive number.

Features of Graphs

The Main Diagonals are y = x and y = –x

y = x runs **UPHILL** from left to right. Points on the line include (1, 1), (3, 3) etc.

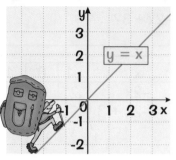

y = –x runs **DOWNHILL** from left to right. Points on the line include (–3, 3), (1, –1) etc.

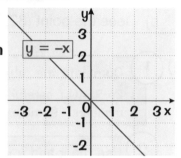

y = 3x, y = 2x and y = –2x go through (0, 0) too

A line that slopes through (0, 0) has the equation 'y = number x'.

The number tells you how steep the line is and a minus sign tells you it slopes downhill.

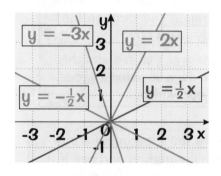

Straight Line Equations are often Written Like This:

$$y = mx + c$$

m is the steepness (or gradient). A negative m-value means a downhill slope.

c is the y-intercept (where it crosses the y-axis)

E.g.

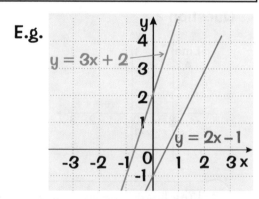

EXAMPLE: Describe the difference between the graphs of these pairs of equations:

a) y = 3x + 1 and y = 2x + 1   y = **3**x + 1 is steeper than y = **2**x + 1.
(Because the m-value is greater.)

b) y = 3x + 1 and y = 3x – 2   y = 3x **+ 1** crosses the y-axis further up
    The c-value here is –2.   than y = 3x **– 2**. (The c-value is greater.)

Learning Objective:

"I understand the main features of graphs and their matching equations."

Features of Graphs

Question 1

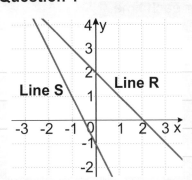

The equation of Line R is y = –x + 2.
Which of the following is the equation for Line S?

A y = –x – 1   **B** y = –2x – 1   **C** y = –2x + 3

1 Compare the <u>gradients</u> of the lines and decide which equations <u>could be correct</u>.

2 Look at where Line S crosses the <u>y-axis</u> and decide which of the remaining equations <u>is correct</u>.

Line S is <u>steeper</u> than Line R, but it's still <u>'downhill'</u>.
Look at the bits before the x's (the m-values):

A y = –x – 1   **B** y = –2x – 1   **C** y = –2x + 3

This equation's graph will have the same gradient as Line R.

These equations have steeper graphs than Line R, but are still downhill.

Line S crosses the y-axis at <u>–1</u>.
Look at the numbers added or subtracted (the c-values):

B y = –2x – 1   **C** y = –2x + 3 ← Crosses the y-axis at 3.

Crosses y-axis at –1.

B is the equation for Line S.

Question 2

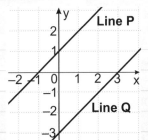

The equation of Line P is y = x + 1.
Write down the equation of Line Q.

1 Compare the <u>gradients</u> of Lines P and Q. This helps you write the <u>first bit</u> of the equation.

2 Look at where Line Q crosses the <u>y-axis</u>. This helps you write the <u>last bit</u> of the equation.

P is y = x + 1
Q has the same gradient as P,
so Q must be <u>y = x + something</u>.

The m-values are both 1.

Line Q crosses the y-axis at –3,
so that must be the 'something':
So Q is y = x + (–3)
or y = x – 3

The something is the c-value.

y = mx + c is definitely the key to understanding equations...

But do remember what m and c are. Another thing that catches people out is forgetting the '–' sign before the m. If the line runs downhill from left to right, m is always negative.

Practice Questions

1   Ben makes a number sequence. He adds the same number each time.
The first 6 terms of Ben's sequence are represented below.

   | | 13 | | | 28 | |

   a)   What is the 6th term in his sequence?

   b)   Write the rule for the nth term of the sequence.

   c)   Use your rule to work out the 100th term of the sequence.

2   Simplify each of these expressions.

   a) $4a + 2b - a + 3b - 7$

   b) $(3 \times 2 \times c) + (7 \times 3 \times d)$

   c) $(4 \times e) + (2 \times e \times 5)$

3   Multiply out the brackets in these expressions and simplify if possible.

   a) $2(f + 3)$

   b) $3(g - 3) + 4(g + 5) + 2$

4   The formula for speed is: speed = distance ÷ time

   A car drives 144 miles in 3 hours. Find its speed in miles per hour.

5   A newspaper article claims that a clown's funniness rating is related to his shoe size
by the formula: $F = 3(4 + S) \div 2S$, where F = funniness rating and S = shoe size.

   Bobo has size 5 feet. Find his funniness rating according to the formula.

6   Look at these two equations: $y = 3x$ and $x + y = 5$

   If these are both true, which two of the following equations are also correct?

   A $y = x - 5$ **B** $4x = 5$ **C** $3x = 5$ **D** $x = 5 - y$

7   Find the value of the letter in these equations.

   a) $6c - 4 = 26$ b) $7(p - 2) = 6 + 6p$

Practice Questions

8   Look at these two equations: $2a + b = 12$ $a + b = 10$

Find the values of a and b that make both equations true.

9   m is a whole number. $5 < 30 - 2m < 11$

Find all the possible values of m.

10   d is a whole number. $10 < d(d^2 + 3) < 50$

 Find all the possible values of d.

11 $x^2(x - 3) = 50$

 Use trial and improvement to find x.

12   Joanna knows that the area of a triangle is 20 cm², and that its height is 5 cm more than its base (b). She wants to use the equation $\frac{1}{2}b(b + 5) = 20$ to find the base of the triangle.

a) Fill in the spaces in the table.

b) What is the base length of the triangle to 1 decimal place?

b	$\frac{1}{2}b(b + 5)$	Too big or too small?
4		Too small
5	25	
4.3		
4.4		Too big
4.35		

13   On squared paper, draw a grid where the x-axis and the y-axis both go from –4 to 4.

a) Add the lines y = 3 and x = –2 to your grid.

b) Write down the coordinates of the point where y = 3 and x = –2 cross.

14   **A** y = x + 3   **B** y = 4x + 2   **C** y = –4x – 2   **D** y = 4x

a) Which one of the lines above goes through point (0, 2)?

b) Which two of the lines above are parallel?

c) Which of the lines goes through points (–1, 2) and (1, 4)?

Classifying Quadrilaterals

Learn the Properties of These Quadrilaterals

Quadrilaterals are 4-sided shapes. The angles in a quadrilateral add up to 360°.

EXAMPLE: Find the missing angle in the quadrilateral on the right.

Add together the 3 angles you know: $x + 120° + 60° + 100° = 360°$
Work out what you need to add to 280° to make 360°: $x + 280° = 360°$
$\underline{x = 80°}$

You need to know the properties of the shapes below.
Make sure that you know how to draw them all too.

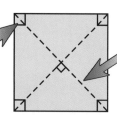

This little square means it's a right angle.

Diagonals go from one corner to the opposite corner.

SQUARE
4 equal-length sides
4 equal angles of 90° (right angles)
2 pairs of parallel sides
Diagonals meet at right angles
4 lines of symmetry
Rotational symmetry of order 4

Parallel sides are always the same distance apart and never meet.

RECTANGLE
2 pairs of equal-length sides
4 equal angles of 90°
2 pairs of parallel sides
2 lines of symmetry
Rotational symmetry of order 2

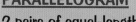

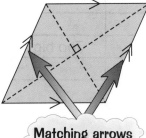

RHOMBUS
4 equal-length sides
2 pairs of equal angles
(opposite angles are equal)
2 pairs of parallel sides
Diagonals meet at right angles
2 lines of symmetry
Rotational symmetry of order 2

Matching arrows show parallel sides.

PARALLELOGRAM
2 pairs of equal-length sides
2 pairs of equal angles
2 pairs of parallel sides
No lines of symmetry
Rotational symmetry of order 2

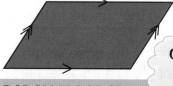

Opposite sides and opposite angles are equal.

TRAPEZIUM
1 pair of parallel sides
No lines of symmetry
No rotational symmetry

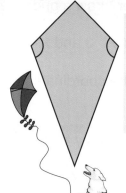

KITE
2 pairs of equal-length sides
1 pair of equal angles
No parallel sides
1 line of symmetry
No rotational symmetry

'Rotational symmetry of order 1' is the same as 'no rotational symmetry'.

Learning Objective:

"I know the properties of different quadrilaterals and can use them to solve problems."

Classifying Quadrilaterals

Question 1

Decide whether the statements below are true or false.

A: A square is a rhombus with angles of 90°.

B: A parallelogram is the only quadrilateral with 2 pairs of equal-length sides.

C: The diagonals of a rectangle cross at 90°.

1 Think about the <u>properties</u> of <u>rhombuses</u> and <u>squares</u>.

2 If you can think of <u>any</u> other quadrilaterals with this property, the statement must be <u>false</u>.

3 Draw a <u>sketch</u> for this one and <u>measure</u> the angles to see if the statement is true.

If all the angles of a rhombus were 90°, it would have four equal sides and four equal angles of 90° — exactly the same as a square. So statement A is <u>true</u>.

Kites also have two pairs of equal-length sides, so statement B is <u>false</u>.

Statement C is <u>false</u>, as you can see from this sketch:

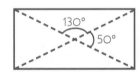

Question 2

Work out the size of angles a and b in this kite.

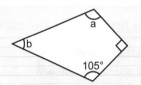

1 A kite has one pair of <u>equal</u> angles — angle a and the angle <u>opposite</u> it, which is 105°.

2 Angles in a quadrilateral add up to <u>360°</u>.

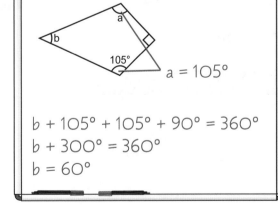

a = 105°

b + 105° + 105° + 90° = 360°
b + 300° = 360°
b = 60°

Learn the properties of all the quadrilaterals...

You need to know their names and how many equal angles, equal sides and parallel sides each shape has. Look out for the little arrows that show you that two lines are parallel.

Angles in Polygons and Parallel Lines

Polygons have Interior and Exterior Angles

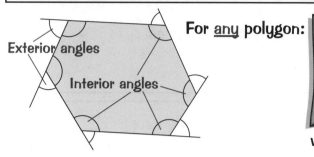

Exterior angles

Interior angles

For any polygon:

SUM OF EXTERIOR ANGLES = 360°

INTERIOR ANGLE = 180° – EXTERIOR ANGLE

SUM OF INTERIOR ANGLES = (n – 2) × 180°

where n is the number of sides (so for a hexagon, n = 6)

For regular polygons ONLY:

• All exterior angles are the same.

• All interior angles are the same.

• Exterior angle = $\frac{360°}{n}$

EXAMPLE: What are the interior and exterior angles of a regular pentagon?

A pentagon has 5 sides, so n = 5.

Exterior angle = $\frac{360°}{n}$ = $\frac{360°}{5}$ = 72°

Interior angle = 180° – 72° = 108°

Angles Around Parallel and Intersecting Lines

When a line crosses two parallel lines...

1) The two groups of angles are the same.

2) There are only two different angles: a small one and a big one.

3) These ALWAYS ADD UP TO 180°. E.g. 30° and 150°

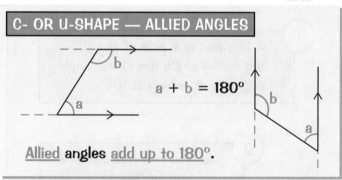

Angles on a straight line add up to 180°.

Look out for these special angles around parallel lines:

F-SHAPE — CORRESPONDING ANGLES

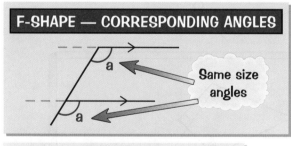

Same size angles

Z-SHAPE — ALTERNATE ANGLES

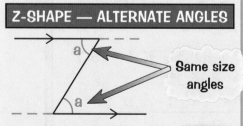

Same size angles

C- OR U-SHAPE — ALLIED ANGLES

a + b = 180°

Allied angles add up to 180°.

Remember, the little arrows mean the lines are parallel.

Learning Objective:

"I can work out missing angles in polygons and around parallel and intersecting lines, and explain my answers."

Angles in Polygons and Parallel Lines

Question 1

Find the size of angle a in this hexagon.

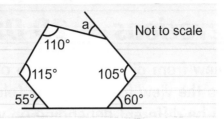

Not to scale

110°
115°   105°
55°   60°
a

① **Find the other <u>exterior</u> <u>angles</u> in the hexagon.**

② **Exterior angles add up to <u>360°</u>.**

For questions like this, there's often <u>more</u> <u>than one way</u> to find the angle you want.

Exterior angle = 180° − interior angle
180° − 110° = 70°
180° − 115° = 65°
180° − 105° = 75°

a + 55° + 65° + 70° + 75° + 60° = 360°
a + 325° = 360°
a = 360° − 325°   ← Subtract 325° from <u>both sides</u>
a = 35°

Question 2

Find the size of angles x and y in the diagram.

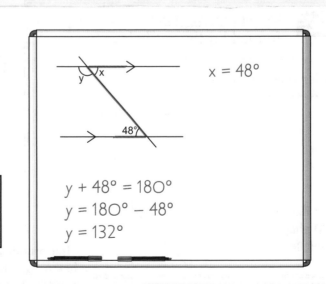

48°   Not to scale

y   x

① **<u>Alternate angles</u> are the same (look out for the reverse <u>Z-shape</u>).**

② **Angles on a <u>straight line</u> add up to <u>180°</u> (you could also use <u>allied angles</u> here).**

y   x

x = 48°

48°

y + 48° = 180°
y = 180° − 48°
y = 132°

Learn all the different types of angles...

You need to know what interior and exterior angles are, and the rules for finding them.
Make sure you learn the proper names for angles around parallel lines as well.

3D Shapes

Plans/Elevations — 2D Drawings of 3D Shapes

A __PLAN__ is the view from <u>directly above</u> an object.

An __ELEVATION__ is the view from <u>one side</u> (elevations are also called <u>projections</u>).

Elevations might be <u>different</u> depending on whether you're looking from the <u>front</u> or the <u>side</u> (like for the triangular prism below).

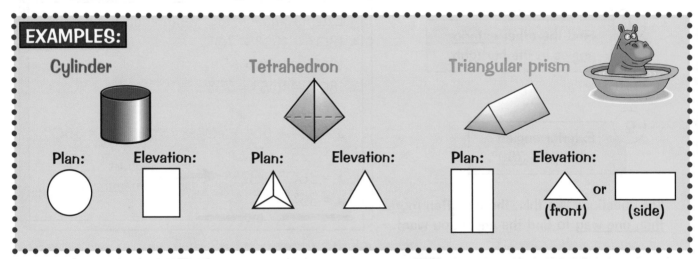

EXAMPLES:

Cylinder   Tetrahedron   Triangular prism

Plan: Elevation: Plan: Elevation: Plan: Elevation:

(front)   or   (side)

Use Isometric Paper to Draw Shapes From Nets

<u>Isometric</u> (dotty) paper looks like this:

<u>Join the dots</u> to draw your shape — you should __ONLY__ draw <u>vertical</u> or <u>diagonal</u> lines (no horizontal lines).

The vertical or diagonal distance between each pair of dots represents 1 cm.

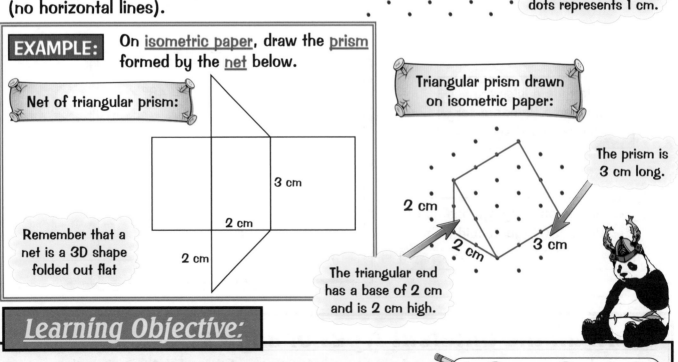

EXAMPLE: On <u>isometric paper</u>, draw the <u>prism</u> formed by the <u>net</u> below.

Net of triangular prism:

3 cm

2 cm

2 cm

Remember that a net is a 3D shape folded out flat

Triangular prism drawn on isometric paper:

The prism is 3 cm long.

2 cm

2 cm

3 cm

The triangular end has a base of 2 cm and is 2 cm high.

Learning Objective:

"I can recognise and use 2D drawings of 3D objects."

3D Shapes

Question 1

Draw a plan and an elevation for the square-based pyramid on the right.

1 The plan is the view from <u>above</u> — just draw what you can see.

2 The elevation of a pyramid is just a <u>triangle</u>.

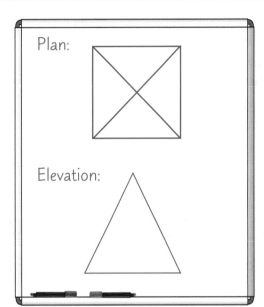

Plan:

Elevation:

Question 2

On a cm grid, draw a net for the prism shown on the right.

1 Start by drawing a big <u>rectangle</u> for the <u>base</u>. Count the <u>dots</u> to work out its <u>size</u> — it needs to be 3 squares long and 2 squares wide.

2 Then draw <u>two faces</u> in the shape of the <u>end</u> of the prism. These should go <u>above</u> and <u>below</u> the rectangle you've just drawn.

3 Finish off the net by adding <u>rectangles</u> for the other sides (you'll need <u>7</u>). They all need to be 1 square by 2 squares.

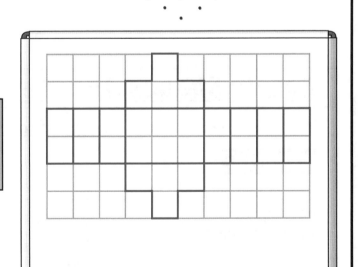

On isometric paper, just join the dots...

For questions about 3D shapes, it sometimes helps to imagine how the net folds up to make the shape — there should be enough faces, and they should all join up.

Transformations

Reflect Shapes in a Mirror Line

Each point and its reflection are exactly the same distance from the mirror line.

EXAMPLE:

Reflect shape A using the y-axis as a mirror line. Label the reflected shape B. Find the coordinates of the image of vertex Z.

The image is just the transformed shape.

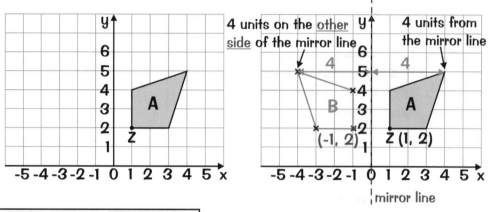

Translate Shapes by Sliding

A translation is a slide — a shape can slide left, right, up or down. A negative number means you move the shape left or down (so a horizontal translation of -2 goes left).

EXAMPLE:

Translate shape C by -4 units horizontally and +3 units vertically. Label the translated shape D. Find the coordinates of the image of vertex W.

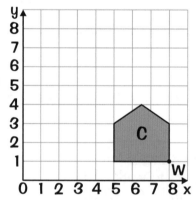

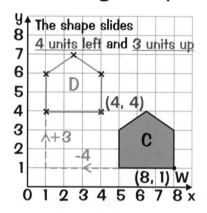

Rotate Shapes About a Point

Use tracing paper to help with reflections and rotations.

You rotate shapes about a centre of rotation (the pivot point).

EXAMPLE:

Rotate triangle E by 90° clockwise about point P. Label the rotated triangle F.

This is the centre of rotation.

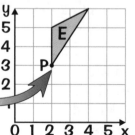

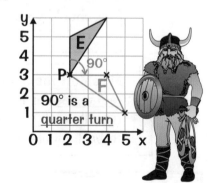

Learning Objective:

"I can reflect, translate and rotate shapes on a grid. I can write instructions for transformations."

Transformations

Question 1

Reflect shape M in the mirror line shown.
Label the reflected shape N.
Write down the coordinates of the image of vertex V.

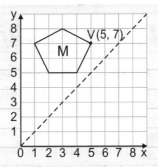

1 From each vertex, measure the <u>same distance</u> on the <u>other side</u> of the mirror line.

2 <u>Join up</u> the points you've drawn.

3 Read off the <u>coordinates</u> of the image of vertex V.

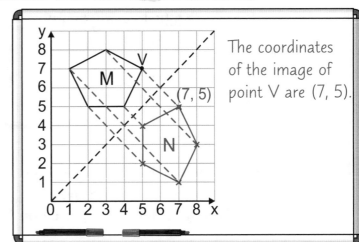

The coordinates of the image of point V are (7, 5).

Question 2

Translate shape J by +3 units horizontally and -2 units vertically. Label the reflected shape K.
Write down the coordinates of the image of vertex T.

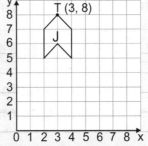

1 Move each vertex <u>3 units right</u> and <u>2 units down</u>.

2 <u>Join up</u> the points you've drawn.

3 Read off the <u>coordinates</u> of the image of vertex T.

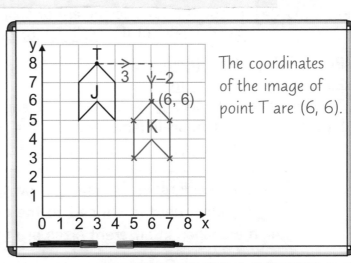

The coordinates of the image of point T are (6, 6).

Using tracing paper can help with transformations...

For these transformations, the transformed shape is identical to the original shape, just in a different position. The posh way of saying this is to say the shapes are <u>congruent</u>.

Enlargement

An Enlargement Changes the Size of a Shape

Enlargements make a shape get bigger — how much bigger depends on the scale factor. Every side of the shape is multiplied by the scale factor.

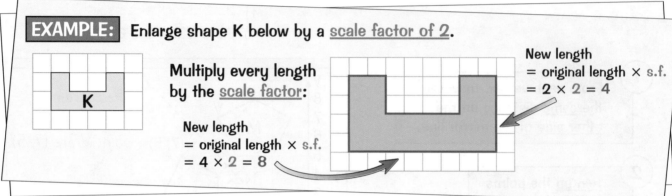

EXAMPLE: Enlarge shape K below by a scale factor of 2.

Multiply every length by the scale factor:

New length
= original length × s.f.
= 4 × 2 = 8

New length
= original length × s.f.
= 2 × 2 = 4

EXAMPLE: A shape has been enlarged by a scale factor of 5.
If the shortest side on the enlarged shape is 15 cm long, how long is the shortest side on the original shape?

1) Each enlarged side is 5 times longer than the original side.
2) So to find a side on the original shape, divide by 5.
3) The shortest side on the original shape is 15 ÷ 5 = **3 cm** long.

Find the Scale Factor by Dividing

You can work out the scale factor by dividing a length on the enlarged shape by the length of the same side on the original shape.

EXAMPLE: Shape B is an enlargement of shape A. Using the lengths given, work out the scale factor of the enlargement.

Base of shape B = **21 cm**
Base of shape A = **7 cm**
To find the scale factor, divide the enlarged length by the original length: scale factor = 21 ÷ 7 = **3**.

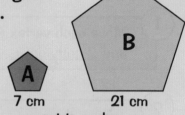

7 cm   21 cm
not to scale

Because enlargements change the size of the shape, enlarged shapes aren't congruent (identical) to the original. Instead, you say that the same shapes in different sizes are similar to each other.

Learning Objective:

"I can enlarge a shape by a scale factor."

Enlargement

Question 1

Enlarge shape P by a scale factor of 3.
Label your enlarged shape Q.

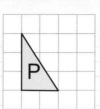

1 Multiply each side length in shape P by 3 (the scale factor).

2 The base of shape P is 2 squares long, so the base of shape Q will be 2 × 3 = 6 squares long.

3 Shape P is 3 squares high, so Q will be 3 × 3 = 9 squares high.

4 Join the two sides to complete the shape.

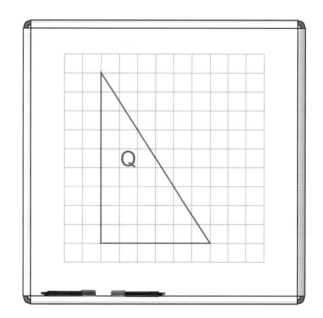

Question 2

Shape W is an enlargement of shape V. The longest side of shape V measures 7 cm and the longest side of shape W measures 70 cm. What is the scale factor of the enlargement?

1 Divide the enlarged length by the original length to find the scale factor.

Scale factor:
enlarged length ÷ original length
= 70 ÷ 7 = 10

The scale factor tells you how big the new shape is...

When trying to find the scale factor, make sure you always do your calculations the right way round — divide the **enlarged** length by the **original** length (not the other way around).

Practice Questions

1   Look at the parallelogram on the right.

    Work out the size of angle x.

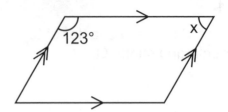

2   The shape on the left is a regular hexagon.

    Find the size of an exterior and an interior angle in this shape.

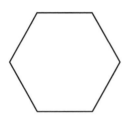

3   The diagram on the right shows parallel lines.

    Find the size of the missing angles a and b.

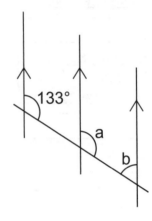

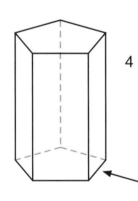

4   The shape on the left is a prism with a regular pentagon end.

    a)   Sketch the plan of the prism.

    b)   Sketch the elevation of the prism from the direction of the arrow.

5   The net of a cuboid is shown on the right.

    On isometric paper, draw the shape this net makes.

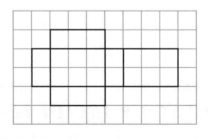

Practice Questions

6   Copy this shape onto a grid with labelled axes.

  a) Reflect the shape in the x-axis.

  b) Write down the coordinates of the image of point R.

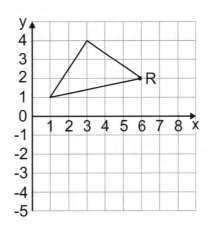

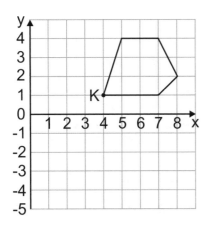

7   Copy this shape onto a grid with labelled axes.

  a) Translate the shape -2 units horizontally and -4 units vertically.

  b) Write down the coordinates of the image of point K.

8   Copy this shape onto a grid with labelled axes.

  a) Rotate the shape 180° clockwise about the point Z.

  b) Write down the coordinates of the image of point G.

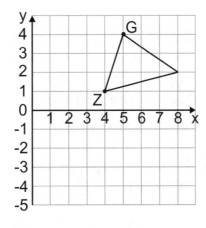

9   Copy this shape onto a grid.

  a) Enlarge this shape by a scale factor of 2.

  b) The same shape is enlarged by a scale factor of 6. What is the length of the top of the enlarged shape?

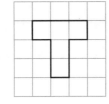

Areas of Compound Shapes

Learn these Area Formulas

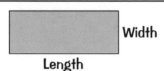

Width
Length

Height

The height is the __vertical height__, not the sloping height.

Base

> Area of a rectangle = length × width

> Area of a triangle = ½ × base × height

Finding Areas of Complicated Shapes

You can find the area of a complicated shape by __splitting__ it up into __simpler__ shapes.

EXAMPLE: Find the area of the shape on the right.

Area of __rectangle__: 4 × 5 = 20 cm²
Area of __triangle__: ½ × 5 × 2 = 5 cm²
__Total area__ = 20 + 5 = 25 cm²

2 cm
4 cm
5 cm

Sometimes you use __subtraction__ to find an area.

2 cm
4 cm
5 cm

__Total area__ = rectangle area − triangle area
= 20 − 5 = 15 cm²

Sometimes area problems have a __letter__ representing a __length__.

EXAMPLE: The diagram shows a square with a rectangle cut out of it.
The shaded area is 88 cm².
What is the value of p?

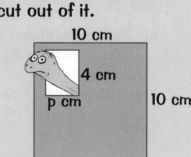

10 cm
4 cm
p cm
10 cm

1 The area of the __outer square__ is:
10 × 10 = __100 cm²__

2 The area of the __small rectangle__ = 100 cm² − shaded area
= 100 cm² − 88 cm² = __12 cm²__

3 The area of the small rectangle is 4 × p or __4p__.
So __4p = 12__   Think: "What times 4 is 12?" "Aha, __3__."   p = 3

Learning Objective:

"I can find the area of a complicated shape
by breaking it down into simpler shapes."

Areas of Compound Shapes

Question 1

Amanda has grey tiles in her kitchen. Each tile has a white flower on it, which is made up of six identical triangles.

Find the area of the grey part of the tile.

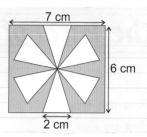

① First find the area of <u>one triangle</u>. You're given the <u>base</u> (2 cm) and can <u>work out the vertical height</u>.

② Use this to work out the area of all <u>six triangles</u>.

③ Work out the area of the <u>whole tile</u> (it's a rectangle, so it's easy).

④ Find the <u>grey area</u> by <u>subtracting</u> the area of the triangles from the area of the whole tile.

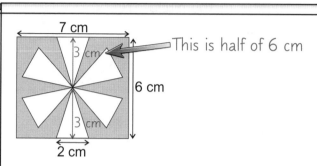

Area of 1 triangle = ½ × base × height
                   = ½ × 2 × 3
                   = 3 cm²

Area of 6 triangles = 3 cm² × 6 = 18 cm²

Area of rectangular tile = length × width
                         = 7 × 6 = 42 cm²

Grey area = 42 − 18 = 24 cm²

Question 2

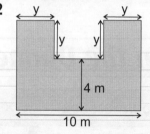

A plan of a room is shown on the left.
Write an expression for the area of the room.

① <u>Split</u> the shape into <u>simple shapes</u>.

② Write an <u>expression</u> for the area of <u>each bit</u>.

③ <u>Add the expressions together</u> to make one big expression and <u>simplify</u> it if possible.

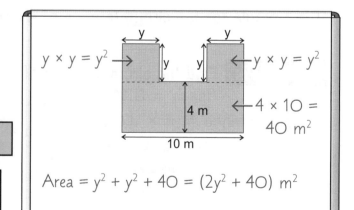

$y \times y = y^2$ →   ← $y \times y = y^2$

          ← 4 × 10 = 40 m²

Area = $y^2 + y^2 + 40 = (2y^2 + 40)$ m²

Rectangles and triangles are your area friends...

Shapes in area questions might look horribly complicated, but you'll always be able to break them down into simple shapes. Then just find the area of the bits and go from there.

Circumference of Circles

Learn the Parts of a Circle and How to Draw them

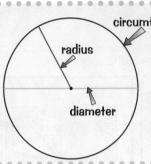

The distance from the <u>edge to the centre</u> of the circle is called the <u>radius</u>.

circumference

radius

diameter

The <u>outside edge</u> of a circle is called the <u>circumference</u>.

The distance <u>across the circle</u> through the centre is called the <u>diameter</u>. The diameter is <u>twice</u> the radius.

EXAMPLE: Draw a circle with a radius of 5 cm.

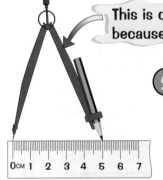

This is called a <u>pair</u> of compasses because it has <u>two</u> 'legs'.

1 Put the <u>needle end</u> of your compasses on the <u>0 mark</u> of your ruler.

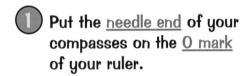

0cm 1 2 3 4 5 6 7

2 Then <u>stretch out</u> your compasses so the <u>tip of your pencil</u> is on the 5 cm mark.

3 <u>Mark a cross</u> on your paper and put the <u>needle</u> of the compasses in the centre of it. Hold the compasses <u>at the top</u> and <u>spin</u> the pencil end around to draw the circle.

Work Out the Circumference from the Diameter

The formula for the <u>circumference</u> of a circle is:

Circumference = π × diameter

EXAMPLE: Find the circumference of this circle.
Use π = 3.14

Circumference = π × diameter
= 3.14 × 4
= 12.56 cm

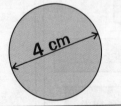

4 cm

π is read as '<u>pi</u>'. It's a <u>decimal</u> starting 3.141592... You'll be told to use a <u>rough</u> value for it such as <u>3</u> or <u>3.14</u>. (Some calculators have a π button for more accurate calculations.)

If you're given the <u>radius</u> of the circle, then <u>double it</u> first to find the <u>diameter</u>.

Learning Objective:

"I can find the circumference of a circle."

Circumference of Circles

Question 1

 Use π = 3.14 to find:

a) the circumference of a circle with a radius of 8 cm.

b) the diameter of a circle with a circumference of 34.54 cm.

a) **1** You're given the <u>radius</u> and you need the <u>diameter</u>. So <u>double</u> it.

2 Now use the <u>formula</u> to find the <u>circumference</u>. You're told the value of π to use in the question.

b To find the <u>circumference</u> you <u>multiplied</u> the diameter by 3.14, so to find the <u>diameter</u> you <u>divide</u> the circumference by 3.14.

a) diameter = radius × 2
= 8 × 2 = 16 cm

circumference = π × diameter
= 3.14 × 16 = 50.24 cm

b) diameter $\xrightarrow{\times 3.14}$ circumference $\xleftarrow{\div 3.14}$

diameter = 34.54 ÷ 3.14 = 11 cm

Question 2

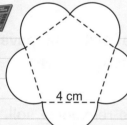

4 cm

This shape is made up of five semi-circles and a regular pentagon. Find its perimeter (use π = 3.14).

1 The distance around each semi-circle is <u>half the circumference</u> of a circle with a <u>4 cm diameter</u>. Find the distance around <u>one semi-circle</u>.

2 The perimeter is made up of <u>five semi-circles</u>, so <u>multiply</u> to find the <u>total perimeter</u>.

Distance around one semi-circle
= (π × diameter) ÷ 2
= (3.14 × 4) ÷ 2
= 6.28 cm

Total perimeter = 5 × 6.28 cm
= 31.4 cm

Circumference is just the distance around a circle...

Don't press down too hard on your compass or you'll end up with a circle that's too big. And before you calculate the circumference, check you've got the diameter, not the radius.

Area of Circles

There's a <u>Formula</u> for the <u>Area</u> of a <u>Circle</u>

The formula for the <u>area of a circle</u> is:

$$\text{Area} = \pi \times (\text{radius})^2$$

Or, just using letters: $A = \pi r^2$

Remember — π (pi) is a decimal that's <u>a bit bigger than 3</u>. You should use whatever <u>approximation</u> a question tells you to. E.g. <u>3 or 3.14</u>.

It doesn't matter if they give you the <u>diameter</u> in an area question. It's <u>DEAD EASY</u> to find the <u>radius</u> — it's always <u>half</u> of the diameter.

EXAMPLE: Find the area of this circle. Use $\pi = 3.14$.

radius = diameter ÷ 2
$\qquad = 4 \div 2 = 2$ cm

$A = \pi \times r^2$
$\quad = 3.14 \times 2^2$
$\quad = 12.56 \text{ cm}^2$

4 cm

A <u>Trickier</u> Circle Area Question

EXAMPLE: Four circles are to be paved on a rectangular area of soil. The paved circles all touch each other and the edge of the rectangular area. They each have a radius of 5 m.

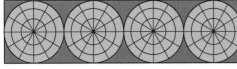

Grass seed is to be sown on the remaining soil. 40 g of seed should be used per m². How much grass seed is needed? Use $\pi = 3.14$.

1) Find the area of <u>one paved circle</u>: $A = \pi \times r^2 = \pi \times 5^2 = 3.14 \times 25 = 78.5 \text{ m}^2$

2) Find the area of <u>all four paved circles</u>: $4 \times 78.5 \text{ m}^2 = 314 \text{ m}^2$

3) Find the area of the whole <u>rectangular area</u>:
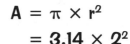
<u>Length</u> = 4 × diameter of one circle = 4×10 m = 40 m
<u>Width</u> = diameter of one circle = 10 m
<u>Area</u> = length × width = $40 \times 10 = 400 \text{ m}^2$

Diameter of circle
= 2 × radius
= 2 × 5 m
= <u>10 m</u>

4) Find area of <u>soil</u>: $400 - 314 = 86 \text{ m}^2$

5) Find <u>grass seed</u> needed: 40 g for 1 m², so for 86 m²: $40 \times 86 = 3440$ g

Learning Objective:

"I can find the area of a circle."

Area of Circles

Question 1

 To raise money for charity, a group of people plan to make the largest plaster in the world.

It is a rectangle with semi-circular ends. Find the area of the giant plaster. Use π = 3.14.

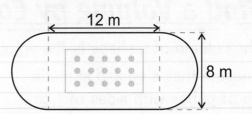

1 Find the <u>combined area</u> of the <u>two semi-circular ends</u>.

This is the same as one <u>whole</u> circle with a <u>8 m diameter</u>.

2 Find the area of the <u>rectangular</u> part of the plaster.

3 <u>Add</u> up the separate areas to find the <u>total area</u>.

Area of circle with 8 m diameter:
radius = diameter ÷ 2 = 8 ÷ 2 = 4 m
$A = \pi \times r^2$
$= 3.14 \times 4^2$
$= 50.24 \ m^2$

Area of rectangular part:
$A = length \times width$
$= 12 \times 8 = 96 \ m^2$

Total area = 50.24 + 96 = 146.24 m²

Question 2

 Dave is making a circular rug with a radius of 2 m. In one day he can complete 2 m². Dave has completed 75% of the rug. To the nearest day, how long has he been working on it? Use π = 3.14.

1 Use the <u>area formula</u> to find the area of the <u>whole rug</u>.

2 Find the area Dave has <u>completed</u>, which is 75% of the whole rug.

3 <u>Divide</u> by the amount Dave can complete in <u>1 day</u> to find out how long it takes him to do <u>9.42 m²</u>.

4 <u>Round</u> the answer to the nearest <u>whole number of days</u>.

Area of whole rug $= \pi \times r^2$
$= 3.14 \times 2^2$
$= 12.56 \ m^2$

Area of rug that Dave has completed:
75% of 12.56 m² = 12.56 ÷ 100 × 75
$= 9.42 \ m^2$

In 1 day Dave can do 2 m².
So 9.42 m² takes 9.42 ÷ 2 = 4.71 days
So to the nearest day, it has taken 5 days.

Double check you're using the right circle formula...

It's very easy to accidentally do π × diameter when you're trying to find the area.
But that won't work at all. It's π × r² you want. Oh, the pitfalls of circle formulas.

Volume

Find a Volume by Counting Cubes

The volume of a shape is the <u>amount of space</u> it takes up.

Imagine that a <u>cuboid</u> is made up of <u>cubes</u> with sides of <u>1 cm</u>. The <u>volume</u> of the cuboid is the same as the <u>number of cubes</u>:

1 cube = 1 cm³

This means 'cm cubed'.

Don't forget about the cubes hidden at the back.

16 cubes = 16 cm³

There's a Formula for the Volume of a Cuboid

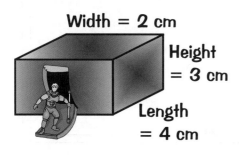

Width = 2 cm

Height = 3 cm

Length = 4 cm

Volume of Cuboid = length × width × height

$$V = L \times W \times H$$

EXAMPLE: Find the volume of this cuboid.

Volume = length × width × height

$$= 4 \times 2 \times 3 = 24 \text{ cm}^3$$

Calculate the Volume of a Prism or Cylinder

A prism has a <u>constant area of cross-section</u> — i.e. the same shape all the way through it.

Volume of prism = cross-sectional area × length

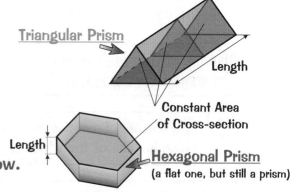

<u>Triangular Prism</u>

Length

Constant Area of Cross-section

Length

<u>Hexagonal Prism</u> (a flat one, but still a prism)

EXAMPLE: Find the volume of the cylinder below. Use π = 3.14.

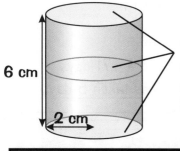

6 cm

2 cm

The constant cross-section of a cylinder is a circle.

1 Area of cross-section: $A = \pi \times r^2$

$$A = 3.14 \times 2^2$$

$$= 12.56 \text{ cm}^2$$

2 Volume = cross-sectional area × length

$$= 12.56 \times 6$$

$$= 75.36 \text{ cm}^3$$

Learning Objective:

"I can find the volume of a cuboid or other prism."

Volume

Question 1

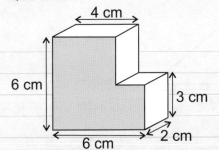

4 cm

6 cm

3 cm

6 cm

2 cm

The shape on the left is made from two cuboids.
Find its volume.

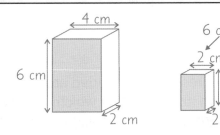

1 Split the shape into the two cuboids. Label their lengths, widths and heights. If any dimensions are missing, work them out.

2 Use the correct formula to work out the volume of each cuboid.

3 Add the volumes together to get the total volume of the shape.

Volume of big cuboid: $V = L \times W \times H$
$= 4 \times 2 \times 6$
$= 48 \text{ cm}^3$

Volume of small cuboid: $V = L \times W \times H$
$= 2 \times 2 \times 3$
$= 12 \text{ cm}^3$

Total volume $= 48 + 12 = 60 \text{ cm}^3$

Question 2

A plastic bead is in the shape of a cuboid with a cuboid-shaped hole through its length.

Find the volume of plastic used to make the bead.

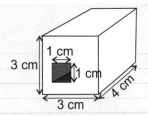

3 cm

1 cm

1 cm

4 cm

3 cm

1 Find the volume of the bead, ignoring the hole.

2 Find the volume of the hole.

3 Subtract the volume of the hole from the volume of the bead to get the volume of plastic.

Volume of bead (ignoring hole):
$V = L \times W \times H$
$= 4 \times 3 \times 3$
$= 36 \text{ cm}^3$

Volume of hole: $V = L \times W \times H$
$= 4 \times 1 \times 1$
$= 4 \text{ cm}^3$

Volume of plastic: $36 - 4 = 32 \text{ cm}^3$

Volume is also known as capacity...

There's often more than one way of working out a volume. E.g. the shape in Q1 is a prism, so you could find the area of the grey side (the cross-section) and multiply by the length.

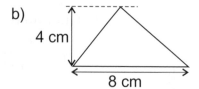

Practice Questions

1   Find the area of these shapes.

a)

10 cm

13 cm

b)

4 cm

8 cm

2   3t + 3u represents the shaded area on the rectangle on the right. Write down an expression which represents the shaded area on each diagram below. Simplify your expressions where possible.

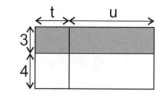

t   u

3

4

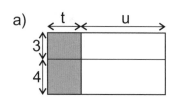

a)

t   u

3

4

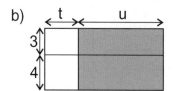

b)

t   u

3

4

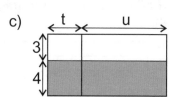

c)

t   u

3

4

3   A plan of the stage for a Primary School nativity play is shown.

 Find its area.

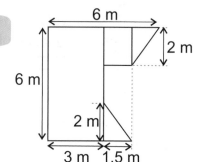

6 m

2 m

6 m

2 m

3 m   1.5 m

4   Kirstie is making a patchwork quilt. One of the pieces is shown on the right. It is a rectangle with four identical triangles removed.

 Find the area of her quilt piece.

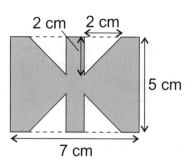

2 cm   2 cm

5 cm

7 cm

5   Find the circumference and area of each of these circles. Use π = 3.14.

a)

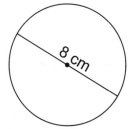

8 cm

b)

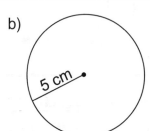

5 cm

Practice Questions

6   A steam roller is flattening a section of road 400 m long.
    Its roller has a diameter of 1.2 m.

 How many **complete** rotations will the roller make as
    it rolls along the section of road? Use π = 3.14.

7   Sue is designing a logo. Her sketch is shown on the right.
    The two circles fit exactly inside the rectangle and do not
    overlap.

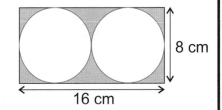

 a)   On squared paper, make an accurate, full-size
         drawing of the logo.

    b)   Find the shaded area on the logo. Use π = 3.14.

8   Fred has 37 centimetre cubes. He builds a cuboid 6 cm by 2 cm by 3 cm.

    How many cubes does he have left over?

9   Max uses 6 identical boxes to build the structure on the right.
    The total volume of the structure is 144 cm³.

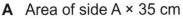

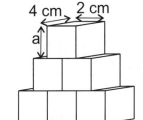 Find the height of the structure.

10 A hen nest box is a pentagonal prism.

    Which of the following will give the volume of the nest box?
    A Area of side A × 35 cm
    B Area of side B × 45 cm
    C Area of side C × 50 cm
    D Area of side D × 60 cm

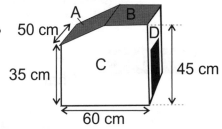

11 Maria has two vases. One is a cuboid
    and the other is a cylinder.

 Which has the greatest volume? Use π = 3.14.
    You must show your working.

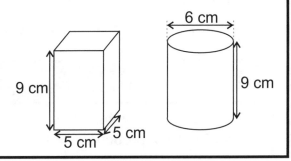

Calculating Probability

All Probabilities are between 0 and 1

You can put the probability of any event happening on a <u>scale from 0 to 1</u>.
The <u>more likely</u> something is to happen, the <u>closer its probability is to 1</u>.

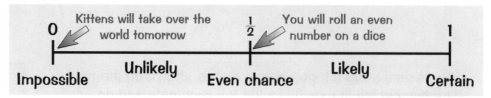

To describe the probability of something happening, look at the <u>number of ways</u>
it can happen and the <u>total number</u> of <u>outcomes</u>.

> **EXAMPLE:** This spinner is <u>equally likely</u> to land on any of the <u>8 sections</u>.

The colour with the <u>most sections</u> is <u>green</u>, so 'green' is the <u>most likely</u> result.

'<u>Blue</u>' is a <u>more likely</u> result than '<u>Red</u>'.

3 of the 8 sections are <u>blue</u>, so you have a <u>3 out of 8</u> or <u>3 in 8</u> chance of getting blue.

That's a <u>probability</u> of $\frac{3}{8}$, or <u>0.375</u>, or <u>37.5%</u>.

Probabilities Add Up to 1

When different results are possible, but <u>only one can happen</u> at a time, these results
are called <u>mutually exclusive</u> events. And there's an <u>important rule</u> about them...

> The <u>PROBABILITIES</u> of <u>all</u> the possible results <u>ADD UP to 1</u>

> **EXAMPLE:** The <u>probability</u> that Sarah will <u>win</u> a badminton match is <u>0.8</u>.
> What is the <u>probability</u> that she <u>won't win</u>?

1) What are the <u>possible results</u>? — 'Sarah wins' and 'Sarah doesn't win'

2) <u>Only one</u> of these can happen, so their <u>probabilities add up to 1</u>. — 0.8 + Probability 'Sarah doesn't win' = 1

3) <u>Subtract from 1</u> to get the answer. — Probability 'Sarah doesn't win' = 1 − 0.8
= <u>0.2</u>

Learning Objective:

"I can work out probabilities
when the total probability is 1."

Calculating Probability

Question 1

a) Using the letters **A**, **B** and **C** at least once, fill in the sections on Spinner 2 so that these statements are true:
- You are equally likely to spin A on both spinners
- You are more likely to spin B than C on Spinner 2

b) What is the probability of spinning A or B on Spinner 1?

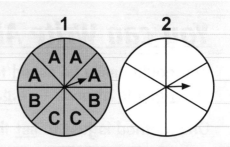

a) ① Work out the <u>probability</u> of getting <u>A</u> on <u>Spinner 1</u>.

② <u>Use your probability</u> to label the '<u>A</u>' sections, then use the <u>second statement</u> to fill in the rest.

b) Count the <u>total number</u> of <u>outcomes</u> and how many of them are <u>A or B</u>. <u>Simplify</u> the fraction if you can.

a) On Spinner 1, 4 of the 8 outcomes are A.
So probability of A = $\frac{4}{8} = \frac{1}{2}$.

So half of the sections on Spinner 2 should be A — and half of 6 is 3. There are 3 sections left, so 2 are B and 1 is C.   E.g.

b) 6 of the 8 outcomes are A or B, so the probability = $\frac{6}{8} = \frac{3}{4}$.

Question 2

A bag contains red, orange, blue and pink counters. Jay selects one counter from the bag. The probabilities of him getting the different colours are shown in the table below.

What is the probability that Jay selects:

a) a pink counter?

b) an orange, blue or pink counter?

Colour	Red	Orange	Blue	Pink
Probability	0.1	0.4	0.2	

a) <u>Only one colour</u> can be selected, so the probabilities of the four colours <u>add up to 1</u>. So <u>subtract</u> the other probabilities from 1.

b) The probability of <u>orange, blue or pink</u> is just the probability of <u>NOT red</u>. So <u>subtract</u> the probability of <u>selecting red</u> from <u>1</u>.

You could also do part b) by <u>adding up</u> the probabilities of orange, blue or pink (i.e. 0.4 + 0.2 + 0.3 = 0.9).

a) Probability of pink
= 1 − 0.1 − 0.4 − 0.2 = 0.3

b) Probability of orange, blue or pink
= 1 − probability of red
= 1 − 0.1 = 0.9

1 is important in probability — that's certain...

If you know all the possible results that can happen, their probabilities have to add up to 1. You might see probabilities written as P(red) — this means 'the probability of getting red'.

Probability — Finding Outcomes

You can Write All the Outcomes in a List

You could easily be asked to <u>find all the possible outcomes</u> from doing <u>two</u> <u>experiments</u> at once — e.g. tossing two coins, or rolling a dice and spinning a spinner.

One method is just to <u>list</u> the outcomes in a <u>logical</u> way.

EXAMPLE: <u>Two coins</u> are tossed together. Write down <u>all the possible outcomes</u>.

1. Start with <u>an outcome</u> from the <u>first</u> coin and <u>match</u> to <u>each</u> <u>outcome</u> from the <u>second</u> coin.

2. <u>Repeat</u> for the <u>other outcome</u> from the first coin.

Coin 1	Coin 2
Heads	Heads
Heads	Tails
Tails	Heads
Tails	Tails

Or, for short...

HH, HT, TH, TT

You can Show All the Outcomes in a Table

Another way to list outcomes from two experiments is to draw a <u>table</u>. <u>Tables work better</u> than lists when there are <u>lots of combinations</u>.

EXAMPLE: I spin this spinner once <u>and</u> roll a six-sided dice. List all the possible outcomes. What is the probability that I get A and an even number?

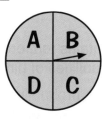

① <u>Draw a TABLE</u>...   ...with the outcomes for the <u>dice</u> along the top...

...and the outcomes for the <u>spinner</u> down the side

	1	2	3	4	5	6
A	A1	A2	A3	A4	A5	A6
B	B1	B2	B3	B4	B5	B6
C	C1	C2	C3	C4	C5	C6
D	D1	D2	D3	D4	D5	D6

② <u>Fill in</u> each square with the <u>letter</u> from the <u>side</u> and the <u>number</u> from the <u>top</u>.

These are the <u>24 outcomes</u>.

To work out the <u>total</u> number of outcomes, you can <u>multiply</u> the number of outcomes from <u>each</u> <u>experiment</u> together — here there are $6 \times 4 = 24$ outcomes.

To get <u>A</u> and an <u>even number</u>, you want A2, A4 or A6. There are <u>3</u> outcomes out of <u>24</u> in total, and all the outcomes are <u>equally likely</u> so the probability is $\frac{3}{24} = \frac{1}{8}$. ($\div 3$)

Lists can get very long — use a table instead.

Learning Objective:

"I can show all the outcomes of two experiments in a diagram, table or list."

Probability — Finding Outcomes

Question 1

The spinner on the right is spun twice.
List all the possible outcomes.

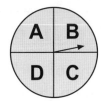

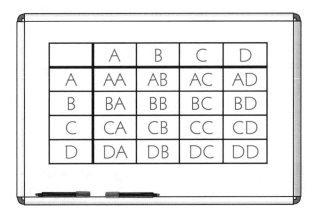

1 Draw a <u>table</u> — put the outcomes for one spin <u>along the top</u> and the other spin <u>down the side</u>.

2 <u>Fill in</u> the <u>outcomes</u> for the <u>two spins</u>.

	A	B	C	D
A	AA	AB	AC	AD
B	BA	BB	BC	BD
C	CA	CB	CC	CD
D	DA	DB	DC	DD

Question 2

Rhiannon rolls a six-sided dice twice and adds her two numbers together to make a total score.

a)   How many possible outcomes are there?

b)   Is Rhiannon more likely to score a total of 5 or 8? Explain your answer.

a)

1 Draw a <u>table</u> — put the outcomes for one roll <u>along the top</u> and the other roll <u>down the side</u>.

2 <u>Add</u> the two numbers together to get the <u>total scores</u> and <u>count how many</u> you've got.

b)

1 All the outcomes are <u>equally likely</u>, so just <u>count</u> the number of times <u>5</u> and <u>8</u> appear in the table.

2 Use your numbers to <u>write an explanation</u>.

a)

+	1	2	3	4	5	6
1	2	3	4	5	6	7
2	3	4	5	6	7	8
3	4	5	6	7	8	9
4	5	6	7	8	9	10
5	6	7	8	9	10	11
6	7	8	9	10	11	12

There are 36 possible outcomes.

b)   <u>Four</u> of the total scores are <u>5</u> and <u>five</u> of the total scores are <u>8</u>. More of the total scores are 8 than 5, so Rhiannon is more likely to score a total of 8.

Outcomes are all the things that can happen...

When you're asked for the outcomes, it means writing down every single combination.
In Q2 above, there are **36** different outcomes even though the scores are repeated.

Frequency Tables and Diagrams

You can Group Data in a Table

Frequency tables show how many of each thing there are. When there are lots of different values, you need to group them into classes (or you'll end up with too many rows). The tricky part is choosing the class intervals to use.

> Frequency means 'how many'.

EXAMPLE: Here are the heights, in centimetres, of 30 penguins. Record this data in a frequency table, using equal-sized class intervals.

> 50, 31, 77, 78, 66, 63, 34, 41, 50, 55, 64, 70, 71, 62, 72, 35, 49, 42, 55, 52, 64, 77, 68, 55, 65, 66, 39, 57, 62, 58

1 Find the lowest and highest values — 31 and 78. So choose equal-sized class intervals that cover all values from 31 to 78 — you need a range of at least 48.

Starting at 30 and grouping into 10's, you can cover the range in five equal intervals — 30 to 40, 40 to 50, ..., 70 to 80.

Height (h) in cm	Tally	Frequency
$30 \leq h < 40$	||||	4
$40 \leq h < 50$	|||	3
$50 \leq h < 60$	ⅢⅢ |||	8
$60 \leq h < 70$	ⅢⅢ ||||	9
$70 \leq h < 80$	ⅢⅢ |	6

> greater than >
> < less than
> greater than ≥ or equal to
> less than ≤ or equal to

2 Write the classes so they don't overlap — each value must only fit into one class.

> $30 \leq h < 40$ means h is greater than or equal to 30, but less than 40.
> So 39 goes in the 1st class, but 40 goes in the 2nd class.

3 Fill in a tally mark for each value and add up the marks to get the frequency for each class. Check the total to make sure you haven't missed any data.

Show Grouped Data on a Frequency Diagram

Frequency diagrams look like bar charts, but there are no gaps between the bars.

A frequency diagram of the penguin data above looks like this. The height of each bar is the frequency of that class.

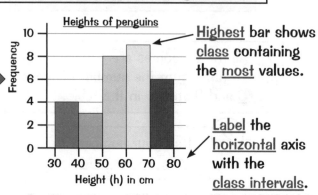

Highest bar shows class containing the most values.

Label the horizontal axis with the class intervals.

Learning Objective:

"I can choose class intervals when using a frequency table. I can understand and draw frequency diagrams."

Frequency Tables and Diagrams

Question 1

Here are the distances, in cm, that 20 children can hop.

30, 40, 99, 62, 38, 22, 50, 56, 104, 70,
72, 41, 45, 69, 77, 80, 43, 41, 57, 78

Complete the frequency table on the right,
using equal class intervals, and fill in the data.

Distance (d) in cm	Tally	Frequency
≤ d <		
≤ d <		
≤ d <		
≤ d <		
≤ d <		

1 Find the <u>lowest</u> and <u>highest</u> values to work out the <u>range</u> to cover.

2 The table shows that you need to split the data into <u>five</u> equal class intervals.
<u>5 × 10 = 50</u>, so groups of 10 won't cover the range.
<u>5 × 20 = 100</u>, so <u>20's</u> will work.

3 <u>Write</u> in the <u>classes</u>. Then <u>fill in the data</u> — cross out each value as you put in the tally mark so you don't count any twice.

Lowest value = <u>22</u>, highest value = <u>104</u>, so need to cover range of at least 83.

5 × 20 = 100, so five groups of 20 will cover the range, e.g. 20-120.

Distance (d) in cm	Tally	Frequency
20 ≤ d < 40	|||	3
40 ≤ d < 60	⊬⊬ |||	8
60 ≤ d < 80	⊬⊬ |	6
80 ≤ d < 100	||	2
100 ≤ d < 120	|	1

Question 2

Here is a frequency diagram showing the heights, in millimetres, of some plants.

How many plants were measured altogether?

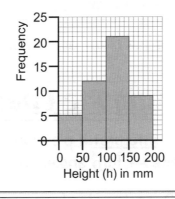

1 The <u>total number</u> of plants equals the <u>total frequency</u>.

2 Find the <u>frequency</u> of each bar and <u>add</u> them up.

Total frequency
= 5 + 12 + 21 + 9
= 47 plants

Frequency for grouped data — how many in a class...

Make sure you know these signs: < (less than), > (greater than), ≤ (less than or equal to) and ≥ (greater than or equal to). You use them to make equal classes covering all values.

Pie Charts

The <u>most important thing</u> you should remember about pie charts is that there are <u>360° in a whole circle</u>.

And that gives you this <u>very important rule</u>.

> TOTAL of everything = 360°

Work Out Angles using a Multiplier

To <u>draw</u> a pie chart, you need to turn <u>numbers of things</u> into <u>angles</u>.

EXAMPLE: This table shows the numbers of different animals in a petting zoo. <u>Draw a pie chart</u> to show the information.

Animal	Geese	Hamsters	Guinea pigs	Rabbits	Ducks
Number	12	20	17	15	26

1 Find the <u>total number</u> of things in the table.

$12 + 20 + 17 + 15 + 26$ = <u>90 animals</u>

2 'Everything = 360°' so find the <u>multiplier</u> that turns your total number into 360°.

<u>Multiplier</u> = 360 ÷ 90 = <u>4</u>

(each animal is represented by 4°)

3 <u>Multiply</u> every number by <u>4</u> to get the <u>angle</u> for each sector.

Animal	Geese	Hamsters	Guinea pigs	Rabbits	Ducks	Total
Number	12	20	17	15	26	90
Angle	12 × 4 = 48°	20 × 4 = 80°	17 × 4 = 68°	15 × 4 = 60°	26 × 4 = 104°	360°

4 Draw your pie chart accurately using a <u>protractor</u> and <u>label</u> each sector.

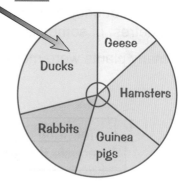

Interpreting Pie Charts

Remember, to <u>interpret</u> a pie chart, you need to do the opposite — <u>turn angles</u> into <u>numbers</u>.

Take the '<u>Geese</u>' sector here...

1) <u>Measure</u> the <u>angle</u> → Geese sector = 48°

2) Turn it into a <u>fraction</u> of the chart → Whole chart = 360°, so fraction of whole = $\frac{48}{360} = \frac{2}{15}$ (÷ 24)

3) <u>Find this fraction</u> of the total number → $\frac{2}{15} \times 90$ animals = <u>12 geese</u>

Learning Objective:

"I can draw and interpret pie charts."

Pie Charts

Question 1

180 people were asked what their favourite colour is. The results are shown in the table on the right.

Draw a pie chart to show this information.

Colour	Number of people
Green	24
Red	40
Yellow	34
Purple	30
Blue	52

1 The question tells you the <u>total</u> number of people — use it to work out the <u>multiplier</u>.

2 Add an 'angle' column to the table. Work out the <u>angle</u> of each sector by <u>multiplying</u> the number of people by your <u>multiplier</u>.

3 <u>Measure each angle accurately</u> using a protractor and draw in the sectors. Don't forget to add <u>labels</u> too.

Total number of people = 180

Each person is represented by 2°

<u>Multiplier</u> = 360 ÷ 180 = <u>2</u>

Colour	Number of people	Angle
Green	24	24 × 2 = 48°
Red	40	40 × 2 = 80°
Yellow	34	34 × 2 = 68°
Purple	30	30 × 2 = 60°
Blue	52	52 × 2 = 104°

<u>Favourite colours</u>

(Pie chart: Green, Red, Yellow, Purple, Blue)

Question 2

Two groups of students were asked what their favourite animal was. The results are shown in the pie charts on the right.

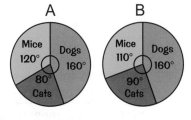

a) What percentage of the students in group B liked cats most?

b) Do the charts show that the same number of students liked dogs most in both groups? Explain your answer.

a Turn the <u>angle</u> for <u>cats</u> into a <u>fraction</u> of the whole circle, then convert it to a <u>percentage</u>.

b Remember — pie charts show <u>proportions</u>.

a) Cats = 90°, $\frac{90}{360} = \frac{1}{4}$ = 25%

b) No, the charts show that the same proportion liked dogs most in both groups. To work out the numbers of students who liked dogs most, you need to know the total number of students in each group.

As I said — the total of everything is 360°

So don't you forget it. That simple fact is the key to all pie chart questions. Make sure you can draw pie charts accurately and interpret them using fractions and percentages.

Scatter Diagrams

Scatter Diagrams _Show_ Correlation

1) A <u>scatter diagram</u> shows whether there is a <u>link</u> between <u>two things</u>. The fancy maths word for this link is <u>correlation</u>.

2) To decide if two things are linked, you need to look at the <u>pattern</u> the points make on the graph. This tells you about the <u>type</u> of <u>correlation</u> and <u>how strong</u> it is.

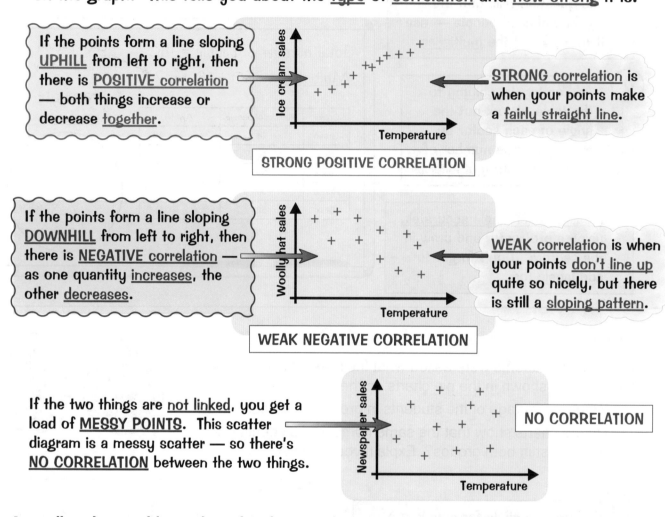

If the points form a line sloping <u>UPHILL</u> from left to right, then there is <u>POSITIVE</u> correlation — both things increase or decrease <u>together</u>.

STRONG POSITIVE CORRELATION

<u>STRONG</u> correlation is when your points make a <u>fairly straight line</u>.

If the points form a line sloping <u>DOWNHILL</u> from left to right, then there is <u>NEGATIVE</u> correlation — as one quantity <u>increases</u>, the other <u>decreases</u>.

WEAK NEGATIVE CORRELATION

<u>WEAK</u> correlation is when your points <u>don't line up</u> quite so nicely, but there is still a <u>sloping pattern</u>.

If the two things are <u>not linked</u>, you get a load of <u>MESSY POINTS</u>. This scatter diagram is a messy scatter — so there's <u>NO CORRELATION</u> between the two things.

NO CORRELATION

As well as being able to describe the correlation, you need to be able to <u>explain what it shows</u> about the <u>two quantities</u>. So for the scatter graphs above:

1) The <u>first diagram</u> above shows <u>positive correlation</u> between <u>temperature</u> and <u>ice cream sales</u>. In other words: The higher the temperature, the more ice creams are sold.

2) The <u>second diagram</u> above shows <u>negative correlation</u> between <u>temperature</u> and <u>woolly hat sales</u>. In other words: The higher the temperature, the fewer woolly hats are sold.

3) The <u>third diagram</u> above shows <u>no correlation</u> between <u>temperature</u> and <u>newspaper sales</u>. In other words: Temperature has no effect on how many newspapers are sold.

Learning Objective:

"I can understand and explain correlation on a scatter diagram."

Scatter Diagrams

Question 1

Describe the <u>type</u> and <u>strength</u> of correlation shown by the scatter diagrams below.

Diagram A

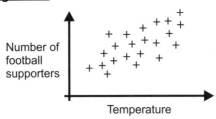

Number of football supporters

Temperature

Diagram B

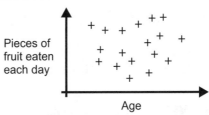

Pieces of fruit eaten each day

Age

1 Look at the <u>pattern</u> of points and decide if there is <u>positive</u>, <u>negative</u> or <u>no</u> correlation.

2 If the diagram shows <u>correlation</u>, decide if it is <u>strong</u> or <u>weak</u>.

Diagram A shows a weak positive correlation between temperature and number of football supporters.

Diagram B shows no correlation between age and pieces of fruit eaten each day.

Question 2

This scatter diagram shows information about Sam's average speed on runs of different lengths.

a) What type of correlation is shown in the diagram?

b) Explain what the diagram shows about the link between Sam's length of run and his average speed.

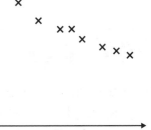

Average speed (mph)

Length of run (miles)

a The points form a fairly <u>straight</u>, <u>downhill</u> line.

b <u>Explain</u> how the <u>two quantities</u> are <u>linked</u>.

a) The diagram shows a strong negative correlation between length of run and average speed.

b) The diagram shows that the longer Sam's run is, the lower his average speed is.

Watch out for sloping lines or messy scatters...

Make sure you know all the right words for describing correlation. And read questions carefully — if you're asked to explain, make sure you say how the quantities are linked.

Conclusions from Graphs

Conversion Graphs Swap Between Units

1) Conversion graphs help you convert between different units
   (e.g. pounds (£) to dollars ($) or miles to kilometres).

2) One unit goes along the horizontal axis and the other goes up the vertical axis.

3) A straight line shows you the rate of conversion
   (e.g. how many dollars you'd get for a pound).

EXAMPLE: The conversion graph on the right converts between miles and kilometres.
Use the graph to work out how many miles 8 km is.

Find 8 km on the km axis, then draw a straight line across to the red line.
Change direction and draw a straight line down to the other axis, and read off the number of miles. So 8 km = 5 miles

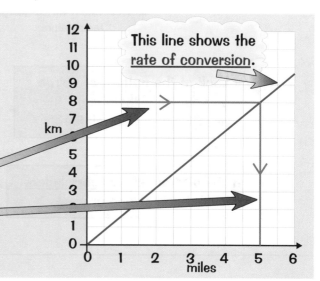

This line shows the rate of conversion.

Don't Be Put Off By Unfamiliar Graphs

If you come across a type of graph you haven't seen before, don't panic.
Just look at what the graph's telling you and what you're trying to find,
then read off the information you need.

EXAMPLE:

The graph on the right shows the dragon tax, based on a dragon's weight and wingspan.
George's dragon weighs 800 kg and has a wingspan of 8 m. How much tax should he pay?

Just look at the graph to find the information you need
— find 800 kg on the horizontal axis and 8 m on the vertical axis and see which region this point is in. It's in the pink region, so George should pay 50 gold pieces in tax.

Dragon tax = 30 gold pieces

Dragon tax = 50 gold pieces

Dragon tax = 70 gold pieces

Dragon tax = 90 gold pieces

Wingspan (m)

Weight of dragon (kg)

Learning Objective:

"I can understand and explain what different graphs show."

Conclusions from Graphs

Question 1

The graph on the right shows the cost of ringing a helpline.
There is a connection fee, then the cost increases with the length
of the phone call. Use the graph to answer these questions.
a) What is the connection fee?
b) Lorenzo makes a call that lasts 4 minutes.
How much will this cost?

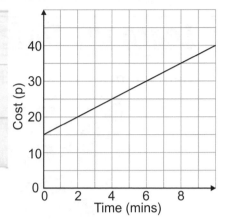

a

The <u>connection fee</u>
is just where the line
crosses the <u>cost axis</u>.

b

Find <u>4</u> on the <u>time axis</u>,
go <u>up</u> to the line, then
<u>change direction</u> and go
<u>across</u> to the other axis.
<u>Read off</u> the cost.

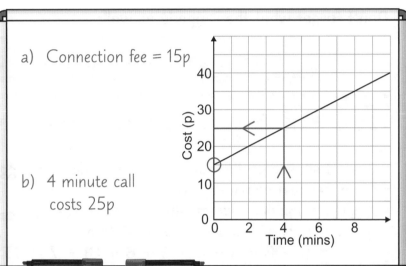

a) Connection fee = 15p

b) 4 minute call
costs 25p

Question 2

The graph on the right shows a company's sales every
month for a year. An advertising campaign started in June.
Summarise the information shown in the graph.

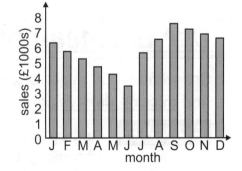

1

Just <u>describe</u> what's
happening on the graph in
as much <u>detail</u> as you can.

Sales were falling from January to June,
reaching their lowest value in June.
After the advertising campaign, sales
started climbing sharply, peaking in
September before falling gradually again.

To interpret a graph, just describe what it shows...

You can get all sorts of different graphs, but even if it's one you haven't seen before, all
you have to do is look at what's on each axis and work out what the graph's showing you.

Averages and Range

Learn the Different Types of Average

I'm mean

Here's a quick recap of the different types of <u>average</u>:

> MODE: <u>most common</u>
>
> MEDIAN: <u>middle value</u> (when the numbers are lined up in order)
>
> MEAN: <u>total</u> of items ÷ <u>number</u> of items

Don't forget what the <u>range</u> is as well:

> RANGE: <u>highest</u> value – <u>lowest</u> value

If there's an <u>even</u> number of values, the median is <u>halfway</u> between the <u>two middle bits</u> of data.

EXAMPLE: Find the <u>mode</u>, <u>median</u>, <u>mean</u> and <u>range</u> for the numbers below:
5, 6, 8, 4, 3, 8, 1

First of all, line up the numbers from smallest to biggest: 1, 3, 4, 5, 6, 8, 8
<u>Mode</u> = most common = 8
<u>Median</u> = middle value = 4th value = 5
<u>Mean</u> = total of items ÷ number of items
    = (1 + 3 + 4 + 5 + 6 + 8 + 8) ÷ 7 = 35 ÷ 7 = 5
<u>Range</u> = highest value – lowest value = 8 – 1 = 7

The middle value is the <u>4th</u> number because there are <u>3</u> numbers on <u>each side</u>.

Use the Mean to Find Missing Bits of Data

Sometimes you might already <u>know</u> the mean of a set of data, and you can use it to find <u>missing data values</u>. You just have to remember the <u>formula</u> for finding the mean.

EXAMPLE: Lindsey is collecting data on the <u>shoe sizes</u> of her friends.
She asks <u>7</u> of her friends what size their shoes are, and the results are:
1, 3, 4, 2, 1, 4, 5. When she includes her <u>own</u> shoe size,
the <u>mean</u> of her results is <u>3</u>. What is Lindsey's shoe size?

Mean = total of items ÷ number of items,
so 3 = (1 + 3 + 4 + 2 + 1 + 4 + 5 + ?) ÷ 8
<u>Multiply</u> both sides by 8 to find the <u>total</u>:
3 × 8 = 1 + 3 + 4 + 2 + 1 + 4 + 5 + ?
So 24 = 20 + ?

You need to add <u>4</u> to 20 to make <u>24</u>, so Lindsey's shoe size is 4.

Learning Objective:

"I can find the mode, median, mean and range and use them to solve problems."

Averages and Range

Question 1

The scores of 6 dogs in a dog show are recorded in the table below.
Mitzi's score is missing. If the mean score was 7, what was Mitzi's score?

Name	Percy	Jolly	Sneezy	Mitzi	Lulu	Wayne
Score	8	9	7		6	5

Use this information to find the mode, median and range of this data.

1 Put the information you <u>know</u> into the <u>formula</u> for the <u>mean</u>.

2 <u>Solve</u> the equation to find the <u>missing value</u>.

3 Put the data <u>in order</u> to find the <u>mode</u>, <u>median</u> and <u>range</u>.

Mean = total of items ÷ number of items
$7 = (8 + 9 + 7 + 6 + 5 + ?) \div 6$
$6 \times 7 = 8 + 9 + 7 + 6 + 5 + ?$
$42 = 35 + ?$
$? = 42 - 35 = 7$
So Mitzi's score was 7.

Rearrange the data: 5, 6, 7, 7, 8, 9
Mode = most common = 7
Median = middle value = 3.5th value = 7
Range = highest − lowest = 9 − 5 = 4

Question 2

Write down three different whole numbers that have a mean of 10 and a range of 6.

1 First work out the <u>total</u> of the three numbers.

2 So now you need to find three numbers that <u>add up</u> to <u>30</u> and have a <u>range</u> of <u>6</u> (you might have to use trial and error here).

Mean = total of items ÷ number of items
So total of items = mean × number of items
$= 10 \times 3 = 30$

$7 + 10 + 13 = 30,$ ← Remember that the three numbers are all <u>different</u>.
and $13 - 7 = 6$.
These numbers have a range of 6 and a mean of 10, so the numbers are 7, 10 and 13.

Sometimes there might be <u>more than one</u> correct answer to questions like this — but in this case, this is the <u>only</u> solution.

Don't get your averages mixed up...

Saying 'the mean of three numbers is 6' is the same as saying 'the sum of three numbers is 18 (= 3 × 6)'. You can use this to help find missing numbers, like in the examples above.

Practice Questions

1   Look at the spinner on the right, and decide
    whether these statements are true or false.

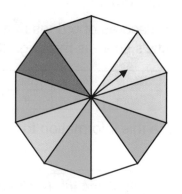

   a)   There is a 50% chance of spinning green.

   b)   It is equally likely that you will spin white or blue.

   c)   The probability of spinning red is 0.2.

   d)   The probability of spinning yellow is 0.1.

2   The probability that Gillian will be late for school is 0.2.
    It is equally likely that she will be on time or early.

    What is the probability that she will be early?

3   Ross has a fair spinner with 4 sections, numbered 1-4.
    He spins the spinner twice and adds together the two results.

   a)   List all the possible outcomes.

   b)   What is the probability that Ross will score more than 7?

4   The data below shows how far, in metres,
    20 children in Class 3 can throw a bean bag.

   2.2, 3.5, 3.4, 1.9, 4.0, 2.9, 4.5, 2.1, 3.1, 3.6,
   4.1, 4.9, 3.7, 2.5, 2.6, 3.8, 4.5, 3.2, 4.8, 2.4

   a)   Use this information to fill in the
        frequency table on the left.

   b)   Draw a frequency diagram to
        show this information.

Distance (d) in m	Tally	Frequency
$1.5 \leq d < 2.0$		
$2.0 \leq d < 2.5$		
$2.5 \leq d < 3.0$		
$3.0 \leq d < 3.5$		
$3.5 \leq d < 4.0$		
$4.0 \leq d < 4.5$		
$4.5 \leq d < 5.0$		

5   120 pupils were asked what their favourite subject was.
    The results are shown in the table on the right.

    Draw a pie chart to show this information.

Subject	Number of people
Maths	15
English	45
Science	12
PE	24
Art	24

SECTION FIVE — HANDLING DATA

Practice Questions

6   The scatter diagram on the right shows information about the time Ishram spends on his homework and the marks he gets.

Write a sentence to describe what the graph shows.

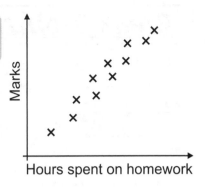

7   The graph on the left converts between degrees Celsius (°C) and degrees Fahrenheit (°F).

a)   Use the graph to convert 10 °C to °F.

b)   Use the graph to convert 82 °F to °C.

8   The graph on the right shows the number of boys and girls doing karate at a leisure centre over a year.

Summarise the information shown on the graph.

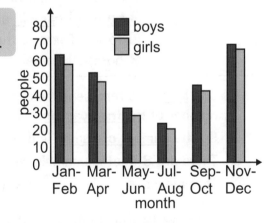

9   Charlie recorded the number of goals scored by his netball team in 6 games. Number of goals scored in the first six games: 5, 8, 2, 3, 4, 5.

The mean number of goals scored per game after 7 games was 4.

a)   Find the number of goals scored in the final game.
b)   Find the mode, median and range of the goals scored in all 7 games.

10   Find four different numbers that have a mean of 12 and a range of 15.

Problem Solving

Break Problems Down into Steps

For some questions, you have to do <u>lots of calculations</u> to get to the answer.
You have to work out what <u>steps</u> you have to do and what <u>order</u> to do them in.

EXAMPLE: Melissa spends <u>£9</u> on ribbon to make friendship bracelets. Pink ribbon costs <u>70p per metre</u>, and she uses <u>6 m</u> of pink ribbon. She also uses <u>8 m</u> of purple ribbon. How much does purple ribbon cost per metre?

STEP 1 Find the <u>total cost</u> of the pink ribbon: ⟶ 70p × 6 = 420p = £4.20

STEP 2 <u>Subtract</u> this from the <u>total amount</u> she spent on ribbon
to find how much she spent on purple ribbon in total: ⟶ £9 – £4.20 = £4.80

STEP 3 She uses 8 m of purple ribbon, so <u>divide</u> this value
by <u>8</u> to find the cost per metre: ⟶ £4.80 ÷ 8 = £0.60
So purple ribbon costs <u>60p per metre</u>.

Use Algebra To Help You Answer Questions

If you're given a lot of <u>information</u> in the question, it might help to write an <u>equation</u> using the information, then <u>solve</u> the equation to find the answer.

EXAMPLE: <u>Dromedary camels</u> have <u>one hump</u> and <u>Bactrian camels</u> have <u>two humps</u>. There are <u>8</u> Bactrian camels at Muddypuddle Zoo. Some <u>mysterious 3-humped camels</u> arrive at the zoo. The camel keepers count <u>32 humps</u> in total. There is the <u>same number</u> of Dromedary camels as mysterious 3-humped camels. How many Dromedary camels are there?

1) Use <u>letters</u> to represent the numbers you don't know: number of <u>Dromedary camels</u> = <u>d</u>, number of <u>Bactrian camels</u> = <u>b</u> and number of <u>mysterious 3-humped camels</u> = <u>c</u>.

2) So the <u>number of humps</u> is $d + 2b + 3c = 32$. ⟵ There are <u>d</u> camels with <u>1 hump</u>, <u>b</u> camels with <u>2 humps</u> and <u>c</u> camels with <u>3 humps</u>, so the number of humps is $d + 2b + 3c$.

3) There are <u>8</u> Bactrian camels, so $b = 8$.

That means
$$d + (2 \times 8) + 3c = 32$$
$$d + 16 + 3c = 32$$

<u>Subtract 16</u> from <u>both sides</u>: $d + 16 - 16 + 3c = 32 - 16$
$$d + 3c = 16$$

4) The number of Dromedary camels is the <u>same</u> as the number of mysterious 3-humped camels, so $d = c$.

So
$$d + 3d = 16$$
$$4d = 16$$

<u>Divide both sides</u> by 4: $4d \div 4 = 16 \div 4$
$$d = 4$$

There are <u>4 Dromedary camels</u> at Muddypuddle Zoo.

Learning Objective:

"I can solve complex problems by breaking them down into smaller tasks."

Problem Solving

Question 1

Freddie makes and sells robots. Giant robots cost £15 to make and he sells them for £25. Super robots cost £18 to make and he sells them for £30. One day, he sells 5 giant robots and makes a total profit of £98. How many super robots has he sold?

1 First, work out the <u>profit</u> he makes on <u>each robot</u>.

2 Find how much profit he makes from selling <u>5 giant robots</u>.

3 Work out <u>how much</u> of the profit comes from selling <u>super robots</u>.

4 Work out <u>how many</u> super robots make this much profit.

Profit = selling price − cost to make

Giant robot: profit = £25 − £15 = £10

Super robot: profit = £30 − £18 = £12

Profit for 5 giant robots = 5 × £10 = £50

Profit for super robots = £98 − £50 = £48

Number of super robots sold = £48 ÷ £12
= 4

Question 2

Uresh makes pots of plants. She has 35 pansies and 45 primroses. She uses 4 plants per pot, and each pot needs 1.5 litres of compost. She uses 80% of her plants. How much compost does she use?

1 Work out how many plants she has <u>in total</u>.

2 Find how many pots she could make if she used <u>all</u> the plants.

3 Work out how many pots she <u>makes</u>.

4 Find how much <u>compost</u> she'll need.

Total number of plants: 35 + 45 = 80 plants

Total number of pots: 80 ÷ 4 = 20 pots

Number of pots made from 80% of the plants:

$80\% = \dfrac{80}{100} = \dfrac{4}{5}$ (÷20)

So 80% of 20 = 20 × $\dfrac{4}{5}$ = 20 ÷ 5 × 4
= 4 × 4 = 16 pots

Compost needed for 16 pots: 16 × 1.5 = 24 litres

Think about what you're trying to find...

Follow this method for real-life questions: read the question and underline the important bits. Decide what calculations you have to do. Do the calculations. Check your answer.

Writing and Drawing to Solve Problems

Put Information into Tables

Sometimes you'll be given a lot of <u>information</u> and told to put it in a <u>table</u>. The table on this page is called a <u>two-way table</u>. Work through <u>each bit</u> of information and <u>fill in</u> the table, then use the <u>Total</u> boxes to <u>check</u> your numbers.

EXAMPLE: Put this information about Class 1 into a two-way table.
1) There are <u>24 pupils</u> in Class 1.   3) <u>15</u> pupils can <u>swim</u>.
2) <u>Half</u> of the pupils are <u>boys</u>.   4) <u>4</u> of the <u>girls</u> can't swim.

First, put the information you're <u>told</u> into the table.
The <u>bottom row</u> shows the <u>total</u> of each <u>column</u>, and the <u>last column</u> shows the <u>total</u> of each <u>row</u>.

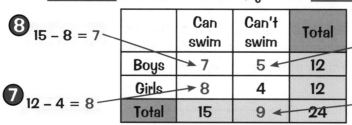

④ 4 girls can't swim.

③ 15 pupils can swim.

② Half of the pupils are boys. Half of 24 is 12. The other half must be girls, so there are also 12 girls.

① There are 24 pupils in total.

	Can swim	Can't swim	Total
Boys			12
Girls		4	12
Total	15		24

Once you know <u>two values</u> in a row or column, you can <u>work out</u> the other value.

⑧ 15 − 8 = 7

⑦ 12 − 4 = 8

⑥ 9 − 4 = 5

⑤ 24 − 15 = 9

	Can swim	Can't swim	Total
Boys	7	5	12
Girls	8	4	12
Total	15	9	24

Draw Sketches to Help Answer the Question

Even if the question doesn't <u>ask</u> for one, you might find it helpful to draw a <u>sketch</u>.

EXAMPLE: Find the <u>area</u> of the outside surface of the cuboid below.

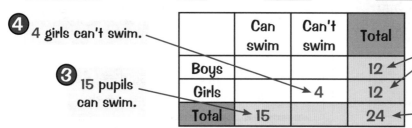

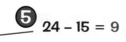

Draw a quick sketch of the <u>net</u> of the cuboid (it doesn't have to be accurate). Remember that the vertical and diagonal gaps on isometric paper represent 1 cm.
Work out the area of <u>each face</u>, then add them together:
$(3 \times 1) + (3 \times 2) + (3 \times 1) + (3 \times 2) + (2 \times 1) + (2 \times 1)$
$= 3 + 6 + 3 + 6 + 2 + 2 = \underline{22}$ cm²

Learning Objective:

"I can show information in different ways, including using diagrams. I can understand and explain information given in different forms."

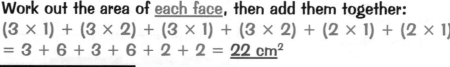

Writing and Drawing to Solve Problems

Question 1

a) Use this information to fill in the two-way table:

1. 27 Year 5 and 6 pupils are asked if they go to drama club.

2. Two-thirds of the pupils go to drama club.

3. One more Year 5 pupil than Year 6 pupils was asked.

4. Half of the Year 5 pupils go to drama club.

	Drama club	Not drama club	Total
Year 5			
Year 6			
Total			

b) Use your table to find how many Year 6 pupils don't go to drama club.

a) **(1)** Put all the information from the <u>numbered points</u> into the table.

4) There are 14 Year 5 pupils in total — half of 14 is 7.

3) You need two numbers that add up to 27 and have a difference of 1 — so that's 14 and 13.

	Drama club	Not drama club	Total
Year 5	7		14
Year 6			13
Total	18		27

2) 2/3 of 27 is 18.

1) There are 27 pupils in total.

(2) Then <u>work out</u> the values that go in the rest of the table.

7) 14 − 7 = 7.

8) 9 − 7 = 2.

	Drama club	Not drama club	Total
Year 5	7	7	14
Year 6	11	2	13
Total	18	9	27

6) 18 − 7 = 11.

5) 27 − 18 = 9.

b Just <u>read off</u> the value you need from the completed table.

b) 2 Year 6 pupils don't go to drama club.

Tables help you show information...

You'll always be able to fill in every space of a two-way table — you might just have to work out other values before you can fill in some of the spaces. Just do it step-by-step.

Giving Justifications

Justifying Means Explaining Your Answer

In the exam, you might be asked to <u>explain</u> your answer. All you have to do is give <u>mathematical reasons</u> to show <u>why</u> you've given that answer.

EXAMPLE: Nina thinks of a number that isn't zero. She <u>doubles</u> it, then <u>subtracts</u> the doubled number from the original number. Will her answer be <u>positive</u>, <u>negative</u> or could it be <u>either</u>? <u>Explain</u> your answer.

Start by thinking about <u>two different cases</u>:

This is often a good starting point.

   1) Nina's number is <u>positive</u>   2) Nina's number is <u>negative</u>

1 If Nina's number is <u>positive</u>, <u>double</u> the number will also be <u>positive</u> (and <u>bigger</u> than the <u>original</u>). She will be <u>subtracting</u> a <u>bigger number</u> from a <u>smaller number</u>, so the answer will be <u>negative</u>. So if her number was 5, $5 - (2 \times 5) = 5 - 10 = -5$.

2 If Nina's number is <u>negative</u>, <u>double</u> the number will also be <u>negative</u>. She will be <u>subtracting</u> a <u>negative number</u>, which is the same as <u>adding</u>. The number she's adding will be <u>bigger</u> than the <u>original number</u>, so the answer will be <u>positive</u>. So if her number was -5, $-5 - (2 \times -5) = -5 - (-10) = -5 + 10 = 5$.

So the answer could be either positive or negative — if Nina thinks of a <u>positive</u> number, the answer will be <u>negative</u>, but if she thinks of a <u>negative</u> number, the answer will be <u>positive</u>.

Use Shape Properties to Justify Answers

If you have a question about <u>shapes</u> and have to explain your answer, use the <u>shape properties</u> to give <u>justifications</u>.

EXAMPLE: Barney draws a <u>triangle</u>. One angle of the triangle measures 112°. Barney says he has drawn a <u>right-angled triangle</u>. Is he correct? <u>Explain</u> your answer.

Use the sum of angles in a triangle.

Barney is incorrect — the angles in a triangle <u>add up to 180°</u>, and a <u>right-angled triangle</u> has one angle of <u>90°</u>. $90° + 112° = 202°$, so his triangle <u>cannot</u> be right-angled.

Learning Objective:

"I can justify my answers by explaining the methods I've used."

Giving Justifications

Question 1

Ramin, Erik and Leah divide a cake between them. Ramin has $\frac{6}{15}$ of the cake, Erik has $\frac{1}{5}$ of the cake and Leah has $\frac{8}{20}$ of the cake. Leah says "I have more cake than Ramin". Is she correct? Explain your answer.

1 Compare the amounts of the cake Ramin and Leah received.

2 Use this to answer the question — don't forget to explain your answer.

$\frac{6}{15}$ simplifies to $\frac{2}{5}$

$\frac{8}{20}$ simplifies to $\frac{2}{5}$

Leah is incorrect — both she and Ramin have $\frac{2}{5}$ of the cake.

Question 2

Lisa draws a quadrilateral with 4 equal sides. Kwan Lam says "the shape Lisa has drawn must be a square". Is Kwan Lam correct? Explain your answer.

1 Think about the properties of quadrilaterals — if you can find another shape with 4 equal sides, Kwan Lam must be wrong.

2 Answer the question — don't forget to explain your answer.

Squares aren't the only quadrilaterals with 4 equal sides — a rhombus also has 4 equal sides. If the shape also has 4 equal angles of 90°, then it must be a square — but we don't know what the angles are so can't say for definite.

Kwan Lam is incorrect — the shape Lisa has drawn could be a rhombus.

Think of reasons for your answer...

You might be given a statement and asked if it's correct or incorrect. If you can find an example that the statement isn't true for, then it must be incorrect.

Practice Questions

1   A teacher spends £60 on books for her class.
    She buys 10 fiction books, which cost £1.80 each.

   She buys twice as many non-fiction books as fiction books.
    All the non-fiction books are the same price. Work out the cost of 1 non-fiction book.

2   Lamar is twice as old as Kali.
    Florence is 3 years younger than Kali.

    The sum of their ages is 29. Find Kali's age.

3   It costs Imogen 10p to make 1 cup of lemonade. She makes 5p
    profit per cup. It costs her 12p to make 1 cup of orangeade.

   One day, she sells 50 cups of lemonade and 40 cups of orangeade.
    She makes a profit of £5.70.
    Work out how much she sells each cup of orangeade for.

4   Raoul needs to buy 25 candles. At the factory, they cost £1.60 each.
    At the supermarket, they come in packs of 5 which cost £10 per pack.

   Raoul has a 10% discount voucher for the supermarket.
    Where should he buy the candles from?

5   Cheyenne is mowing the lawn of a stately home. The lawn
    measures 50 m by 40 m. After 1 hour, she has mown 250 m².

    How many hours will it take her to mow the entire lawn?

6   Tilly builds a tower out of wooden blocks. All red blocks are identical and all blue blocks
    are identical. She makes one tower using 6 red blocks. The tower is 42 cm tall.
    She makes another tower using 4 red blocks and 2 blue blocks. This tower is 38 cm tall.

    Find the height of each type of block.

Practice Questions

7   A snail is climbing up an electricity pylon. Every day, it crawls
     2.5 m up the pylon, but each night it slides down 0.5 m.

     The pylon is 20 m tall. How many days will it take
     for the snail to reach the top?

8   Use the information below to complete the table on the right.

     • 60 pupils go on a school trip.
     • One third of the pupils are Infants,
       the rest are Juniors.
     • Half of the pupils go to the castle,
       the rest go to the museum.
     • Three quarters of the Infants go to the castle.

	Castle	Museum	Total
Infants			
Juniors			
Total			

9   One side of a parallelogram measures 12 cm.
     The perimeter of the parallelogram is 40 cm.

     Work out the lengths of the other three sides of the parallelogram.

10   The formula for the nth term of a sequence is $4n - 3$.
     Johanna says "all the terms in this sequence are positive".

     Is Johanna correct? Explain your answer.

11   Manu, Mike and Owen can only see one corner
     of a triangle (shown on the right).

     Manu says "the triangle could be right-angled".
     Mike says "the triangle could be isosceles".
     Owen says "the triangle could be equilateral".

     Which boys are correct? Explain your answer.

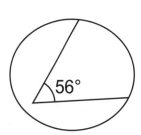

12   Aalim thinks of a number. He squares it, then adds on 5.

     Is his answer positive, negative or could it be either? Explain your answer.

Answers

Pages 14-15 — Section One

1) The factors of 28 are: 1, 2, 4, 7, 14, 28
   The factors of 42 are: 1, 2, 3, 6, 7, 14, 21, 42
   So the common factors of 28 and 42 are:
   1, 2, 7, 14. 2 and 7 are prime numbers,
   so Izzy's number must be **14**.

2) a) $-10 \times 13 = \textbf{-130}$
   b) $-54 \div \textbf{-9} = 6$
   c) $\textbf{7} \times -7 = -49$
   You need to remember the rules for multiplying and dividing with negative numbers for this question.

3) a) The difference between the numbered marks is
   $6.25 - 6.2 = 0.05$. There are 5 small steps from
   6.2 to 6.25, so each small step is $0.05 \div 5 = 0.01$.
   Count on 2 steps of 0.01 from 6.25 to the arrow:
   $6.25 + 2 \times 0.01 = \textbf{6.27}$
   b) There are 10 small steps between −500 000 and 0,
   so each small step is worth $500\,000 \div 10 = 50\,000$.
   Count back 7 steps of 50 000 from 0:
   $0 - 7 \times 50\,000 = \textbf{-350 000}$

4) $4 = 12 \div 3$, so the number on the bottom of the
   first fraction is $15 \div 3 = \textbf{5}$. $60 = 15 \times 4$, so the
   number on top of the third fraction is $12 \times 4 = \textbf{48}$.
   $$\frac{4}{\boxed{5}} = \frac{12}{15} = \frac{\boxed{48}}{60}$$
   Remember, for equivalent fractions, you always do the same thing to the top and the bottom.

5) Compare the amounts by turning 70% into a
   fraction: $70\% = \dfrac{7}{10}$
   Find a common denominator for $\dfrac{11}{15}$ and $\dfrac{7}{10}$.
   30 is a multiple of 15 and 10, so:
   $$\frac{11}{15} = \frac{11 \times 2}{15 \times 2} = \frac{22}{30} \quad \text{and} \quad \frac{7}{10} = \frac{7 \times 3}{10 \times 3} = \frac{21}{30}$$
   $\dfrac{22}{30} > \dfrac{21}{30}$ so $\dfrac{11}{15} > 70\%$
   So **Rupinder** sold the most tickets.

6) Total fraction of red and white tulips $= \dfrac{1}{7} + \dfrac{4}{9}$
   Use 63 as a common denominator:
   $$\frac{1}{7} = \frac{1 \times 9}{7 \times 9} = \frac{9}{63} \quad \text{and} \quad \frac{4}{9} = \frac{4 \times 7}{9 \times 7} = \frac{28}{63}$$
   So $\dfrac{1}{7} + \dfrac{4}{9} = \dfrac{9}{63} + \dfrac{28}{63} = \dfrac{9 + 28}{63} = \dfrac{\textbf{37}}{\textbf{63}}$

7) a) Turn the mixed numbers into improper fractions:
   $$3\frac{1}{2} = \frac{6}{2} + \frac{1}{2} = \frac{7}{2} \qquad 2\frac{1}{5} = \frac{10}{5} + \frac{1}{5} = \frac{11}{5}$$
   Now put them over a common denominator.
   10 is a multiple of 2 and 5, so:
   $$\frac{7}{2} = \frac{7 \times 5}{2 \times 5} = \frac{35}{10} \quad \text{and} \quad \frac{11}{5} = \frac{11 \times 2}{5 \times 2} = \frac{22}{10}$$
   Use the improper fractions to do the addition:
   $$3\frac{1}{2} + 2\frac{1}{5} = \frac{35}{10} + \frac{22}{10} = \frac{35 + 22}{10}$$
   $$= \frac{57}{10} = \frac{50}{10} + \frac{7}{10} = \textbf{5}\frac{\textbf{7}}{\textbf{10}}$$

b) Turn the mixed numbers into improper fractions:
   $$8\frac{1}{10} = \frac{80}{10} + \frac{1}{10} = \frac{81}{10}$$
   $$2\frac{3}{4} = \frac{8}{4} + \frac{3}{4} = \frac{11}{4}$$
   Now put them over a common denominator.
   20 is a multiple of 10 and 4, so:
   $$\frac{81}{10} = \frac{81 \times 2}{10 \times 2} = \frac{162}{20} \quad \text{and} \quad \frac{11}{4} = \frac{11 \times 5}{4 \times 5} = \frac{55}{20}$$
   Use the improper fractions to do the subtraction:
   $$8\frac{1}{10} - 2\frac{3}{4} = \frac{162}{20} - \frac{55}{20} = \frac{162 - 55}{20}$$
   $$= \frac{107}{20} = \frac{100}{20} + \frac{7}{20} = \textbf{5}\frac{\textbf{7}}{\textbf{20}}$$

8) Percentage of chocolate biscuits $= 100\% - 55\%$
   $= 45\%$
   So number of chocolate biscuits $= 240 \times 45\%$
   $$= 240 \times \frac{45}{100} = 240 \times \frac{9}{20}$$
   $$= (240 \div 20) \times 9 = 12 \times 9$$
   $= \textbf{108 chocolate biscuits}$

9) Size of the loss $= £75 - £57 = £18$
   Percentage loss $= \dfrac{£18}{£75} = \dfrac{6}{25} = \dfrac{24}{100} = \textbf{24\%}$

10) 6 capes need 7.2 m of fabric
   so 1 cape needs $7.2 \text{ m} \div 6 = 1.2 \text{ m}$
   so 8 capes will need $1.2 \text{ m} \times 8 = \textbf{9.6 m}$

11) $10 + 5 + 3 = 18$, so there are 18 parts in the ratio.
   $180 \div 18 = 10$, so each part is 10 gold coins.
   So Penny gets $10 \times 10 = \textbf{100 gold coins}$,
   Luc gets $5 \times 10 = \textbf{50 gold coins}$
   and Kelsey gets $3 \times 10 = \textbf{30 gold coins}$.

12) Ratio of lions : zebras
   $= 14 : 42$
   $= 7 : 21$ (dividing by 2)
   $= \textbf{1 : 3}$ (dividing by 7)

Pages 30-31 — Section Two

1) a) The difference between the 2nd and 5th terms is
   $28 - 13 = 15$. There are 3 steps between these
   terms, so each step is $15 \div 3 = 5$.
   6th term $= 28 + 5 = \textbf{33}$
   b) The difference is 5, so compare the terms to the
   5 times table:
   5 times table: 5,   10,   15,   20,   25,   30
   Sequence terms: _,   13,   _,   _,   28,   33
   The terms are 3 more than the corresponding times
   table numbers, so the rule is:
   Multiply n by 5 and add 3, or 5n + 3
   c) 100th term $= 5 \times 100 + 3 = \textbf{503}$

2) a) $4a + 2b - a + 3b - 7 = (4a - a) + (2b + 3b) - 7$
   $\qquad\qquad\qquad\qquad\qquad = \textbf{3a + 5b − 7}$
   b) $(3 \times 2 \times c) + (7 \times 3 \times d) = \textbf{6c + 21d}$
   c) $(4 \times e) + (2 \times e \times 5) = 4e + 10e = \textbf{14e}$

3) a) $2(f + 3) = (2 \times f) + (2 \times 3) = \textbf{2f + 6}$
   b) $3(g − 3) + 4(g + 5) + 2$
   $= (3 \times g) + (3 \times -3) + (4 \times g) + (4 \times 5) + 2$
   $= 3g − 9 + 4g + 20 + 2 = \textbf{7g + 13}$

Answers

4)   speed = distance ÷ time = 144 miles ÷ 3 hours
     = **48 miles per hour**

5) $S = 5$, so
     $F = 3(4 + S) ÷ 2S$
       $= 3(4 + 5) ÷ (2 × 5)$
       $= 3 × 9 ÷ 10$
       $= 27 ÷ 10$
       = **2.7**

6)   Substituting $y = 3x$ in $x + y = 5$ gives:
     $x + 3x = 5 \Rightarrow 4x = 5$ **Equation B is correct**
     $x + y = 5$, so $x + y - y = 5 - y \Rightarrow x = 5 - y$
     Equation D is correct
     It might help to think about how you'd rearrange
     $x + y = 5$ if it contained numbers:
     E.g. $2 + 3 = 5 \Rightarrow 2 = 5 - 3$.

7) a) $6c - 4 = 26 \Rightarrow 6c - 4 + 4 = 26 + 4$
              $6c = 30$
            $6c ÷ 6 = 30 ÷ 6$
               c = 5

   b) $7(p - 2) = 6 + 6p$
      $(7 × p) + (7 × -2) = 6 + 6p$
      $7p - 14 = 6 + 6p$
      $7p - 14 + 14 = 6 + 6p + 14$
      $7p = 20 + 6p$
      $7p - 6p = 20 + 6p - 6p$
      $p = 20$

8) $2a + b = 12 \Rightarrow a + a + b = 12$
     and $a + b = 10$
     so $a + 10 = 12 \Rightarrow a = 12 - 10 = 2$
     Substitute $a = 2$ into $a + b = 10$:
     $2 + b = 10 \Rightarrow b = 10 - 2 = 8$
     a = 2, b = 8

9)   Try $m = 10$: $30 - (2 × 10) = 30 - 20 = 10$
     This is greater than 5 but less than 11,
     so 10 is a possible value of m.
     Try $m = 11$: $30 - (2 × 11) = 30 - 22 = 8$
     This is greater than 5 but less than 11,
     so 11 is a possible value of m.
     Try $m = 12$: $30 - (2 × 12) = 30 - 24 = 6$
     This is greater than 5 but less than 11,
     so 12 is a possible value of m.
     Try $m = 13$: $30 - (2 × 13) = 30 - 26 = 4$
     This isn't greater than 5,
     so 13 is not a possible value of m.
     Going the other way from $m = 10$:
     Try $m = 9$: $30 - (2 × 9) = 30 - 18 = 12$
     This isn't less than 11,
     so 9 is not a possible value of m.
     Possible values of m are 10, 11 and 12.

10) Try $d = 2$: $2(2^2 + 3) = 2(4 + 3) = 2 × 7 = 14$
     This is greater than 10 but less than 50,
     so 2 is a possible value of d.
     Try $d = 3$: $3(3^2 + 3) = 3(9 + 3) = 3 × 12 = 36$
     This is greater than 10 but less than 50,
     so 3 is a possible value of d.
     Try $d = 4$: $4(4^2 + 3) = 4(16 + 3) = 4 × 19 = 76$
     This isn't less than 50, so 4 isn't a possible value of d.

Going the other way from $d = 2$:
Try $d = 1$: $1(1^2 + 3) = 1(1 + 3) = 1 × 4 = 4$
This isn't greater than 10,
so 1 isn't a possible value of d.
Possible values of d are 2 and 3.

11) E.g.

x	$x^2(x - 3)$	Too big or too small?
6	$6^2(6 - 3) = 36 × 3 = 108$	Too big
5	$5^2(5 - 3) = 25 × 2 = 50$	Perfect

    x = 5

12) a)

b	$\frac{1}{2}b(b + 5)$	Too big / too small?
4	$\frac{1}{2} × 4 × (4 + 5) = 18$	Too small
5	25	Too big
4.3	$\frac{1}{2} × 4.3 × (4.3 + 5) = 19.995$	Too small
4.4	$\frac{1}{2} × 4.4 × (4.4 + 5) = 20.68$	Too big
4.35	$\frac{1}{2} × 4.35 × (4.35 + 5) = 20.33625$	Too big

  b) **4.3**
    From the table, you know the exact value is between
    4.3 and 4.35, so it must be 4.3 to 1 decimal place.

13) a)

  b) **(–2, 3)**

14) a) **B**
    In equation B, when $x = 0$, $y = 0 + 2 = 2$,
    so it passes through the point (0, 2).

  b) **B and D**
    Parallel lines have the same slope, and the m-value
    tells you what this is. $y = 4x + 2$ and $y = 4x$ have the
    same m-value so they're parallel.

  c) **A**
    Put the x-value of each point into the equation for the
    line — if it's on the line, it will give you the y-value for
    that point.

Answers

Pages 42-43 — Section Three

1) Parallelograms have two pairs of equal angles, and the angles in a quadrilateral add up to 360°, so 123° + 123° + x + x = 360°.
246° + 2x = 360°
2x = 114°
x = **57°**
You could have also used the properties of parallel lines for this question — allied angles add up to 180°, so 123° + x = 180°.

2) In a regular polygon, all the exterior angles are the same and can be found using the formula:
Exterior angle = $\frac{360°}{n} = \frac{360°}{6} = $ **60°**
All the interior angles are the same, and can be found using the formula:
Interior angle = 180° – exterior angle
= 180° – 60° = **120°**

3) Corresponding angles are equal, so a = **133°**.
Allied angles add up to 180°,
so b = 180° – a = 180° – 133° = **47°**

4) a) Plan:
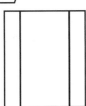
b) Elevation:

5)

6) a)
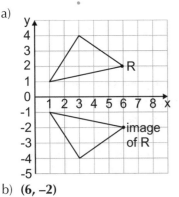
b) **(6, –2)**

7) a)
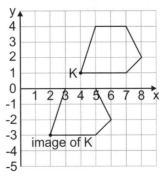
b) **(2, –3)**

8) a)
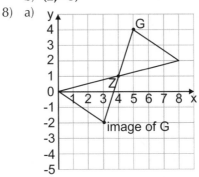
b) **(3, –2)**

9) a)
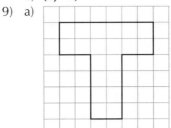
b) Top of original shape = 3 squares
Top of enlarged shape = 3 × 6 = **18 squares**

Pages 52-53 — Section Four

1) a) 13 × 10 = **130 cm²**
b) $\frac{1}{2}$(8 × 4) = **16 cm²**

2) a) (3 × t) + (4 × t) = 3t + 4t = **7t**
b) (3 × u) + (4 × u) = 3u + 4u = **7u**
c) (4 × t) + (4 × u) = **4t + 4u**

3) Area of large rectangle = 6 × 3 = 18 m²
Area of small rectangle = 2 × 1.5 = 3 m²
Width of top triangle = 6 – 3 – 1.5 = 1.5 m, so both triangles are identical.
Area of one triangle = $\frac{1}{2}$(2 × 1.5) = 1.5 m²
Area of two triangles = 2 × 1.5 = 3 m²
Total area = 18 + 3 + 3 = **24 m²**

4) Area of rectangle (ignoring removed triangles)
= 7 × 5 = 35 cm²
Area of one removed triangle = $\frac{1}{2}$(2 × 2) = 2 cm²
Area of four removed triangles = 4 × 2 = 8 cm²
Area of quilt piece = 35 – 8 = **27 cm²**

5) a) Circumference = π × diameter = 3.14 × 8
= **25.12 cm**
Radius = diameter ÷ 2 = 8 ÷ 2 = 4 cm
Area = π × r² = 3.14 × 4² = 3.14 × 16 = **50.24 cm²**

Answers

b) Diameter = radius × 2 = 5 × 2 = 10 cm
Circumference = π × diameter = 3.14 × 10 =
31.4 cm
Area = π × r² = 3.14 × 5² = 3.14 × 25 = **78.5 cm²**

6) Circumference of roller = π × diameter
= 3.14 × 1.2 = 3.768 m
Number of rotations = 400 ÷ 3.768 = 106.157...
= **106 complete rotations**
*Watch out for these wheel questions. For every
full rotation, the wheel travels a distance equal to
its circumference.*

7) a)

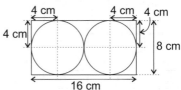

Not full size.
*The trick is to find exactly where the circle centres
should be — you put your compass point where
the dashed lines cross.*

b) Area of rectangle = 16 × 8 = 128 cm²
Area of 2 circles = 2 × π × r²
= 2 × 3.14 × 4²
= 2 × 3.14 × 16 = 100.48 cm²
Shaded area = 128 − 100.48 = **27.52 cm²**

8) Volume of 6 cm by 2 cm by 3 cm cuboid
= 6 × 2 × 3 = 36 cm³
(This is the same as the number of cm cubes.)
Cubes left over = 37 − 36 = **1**

9) Volume of each cube = 144 ÷ 6 = 24 cm³
so 4 × 2 × a = 24
8 × a = 24
a = 24 ÷ 8 = 3 cm
The structure is 3 blocks high:
3 × a = 3 × 3 = **9 cm**

10) **C**
*Side C is the cross-section of the prism — it goes
all the way through the shape. The volume of a
prism is the cross-section multiplied by the length
of the prism.*

11) Volume of cuboid = 9 × 5 × 5 = 225 cm³
Radius of cylinder = diameter ÷ 2 = 6 ÷ 2 = 3 cm
Volume of cylinder
= area of cross-section × length
= (π × r²) × length
= 3.14 × 3² × 9
= 3.14 × 9 × 9 = 254.34 cm³
Volume of cylinder is greater.

Pages 68-69 — Section Five

1) a) **False** — there are 4 green sections out of 10 in
total, so this is not a 50% chance.
b) **True** — there are 2 sections each of white
and blue.
c) **False** — there are no red sections on the spinner,
so the probability of spinning red is 0.

d) **True** — there is 1 yellow section out of 10,
so the probability of spinning yellow is 1/10 = 0.1.

2) Probability 'Gillian is early or on time'
= 1 − probability 'Gillian is late' = 1 − 0.2 = 0.8.
Probability 'Gillian is early'
= probability 'Gillian is early or on time' ÷ 2
= 0.8 ÷ 2 = **0.4**.

3) a)

+	1	2	3	4
1	2	3	4	5
2	3	4	5	6
3	4	5	6	7
4	5	6	7	8

b) Only 1 outcome out of 16 that's more than 7 (8), so
the probability that Ross scores more than 7 is $\frac{1}{16}$.

4) a)

Distance (d) in m	Tally	Frequency
1.5 ≤ d < 2.0	I	1
2.0 ≤ d < 2.5	III	3
2.5 ≤ d < 3.0	III	3
3.0 ≤ d < 3.5	III	3
3.5 ≤ d < 4.0	IIII	4
4.0 ≤ d < 4.5	II	2
4.5 ≤ d < 5.0	IIII	4

b)

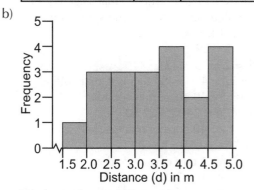

5) Work out the angle for each sector.
360 ÷ 120 = 3, so the multiplier is 3.
Maths: 15 × 3 = 45°   English: 45 × 3 = 135°
Science: 12 × 3 = 36°   PE: 24 × 3 = 72°
Art: 24 × 3 = 72°

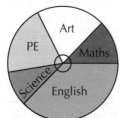

6) The graph shows **strong positive correlation**
— the **longer** Ishram spends on his homework,
the **more marks** he gets.

7) a) 10 °C = **50 °F**
b) 82 °F = **28 °C**

8) The number of people doing karate **falls** from the
start of the year, with lowest numbers during the
summer months, then **increases** towards the end of
the year. More **boys** than girls do karate.

Answers

9) a) Mean = total of items ÷ number of items
$4 = (5 + 8 + 2 + 3 + 4 + 5 + ?) ÷ 7$
$4 = (27 + ?) ÷ 7$
$7 × 4 = 27 + ?$
$28 = 27 + ?$
$? = 28 – 27 = 1$
So **1 goal** was scored in the final game.

   b) Line all the data up in order: 1, 2, 3, 4, 5, 5, 8
Mode = **5**, median = **4** and range = 8 – 1 = **7**

10) $12 × 4 = 48$, so the four numbers must add up to 48 and have a range of 15.
E.g. **6, 10, 11, 21** (range = 21 – 6 = 15,
mean = 6 + 10 + 11 + 21 ÷ 4 = 48 ÷ 4 = 12)
There's more than one correct answer here (for example, 6, 9, 12 and 21 also works). You might have got a different answer, but as long as you have four different numbers that add up to 48 and have a range of 15 you'll be right.

Pages 76-77 — Section Six

1) Total cost of fiction books: $10 × £1.80 = £18$
Total spent on non-fiction books: $£60 – £18 = £42$
Number of non-fiction books bought: $10 × 2 = 20$
Cost of 1 non-fiction book: $£42 ÷ 20 = **£2.10**$.

2) Call Kali's age k. Then Lamar's age is 2k and Florence's age is k – 3. The sum of their ages is 29,
so $2k + k + (k – 3) = 29$
$4k – 3 = 29$
$4k = 29 + 3 = 32$
$k = 32 ÷ 4 = 8$. So Kali is **8 years old**.

3) Profit for 50 cups of lemonade:
$50 × 5p = 250p = £2.50$.
Profit for 40 cups of orangeade:
$£5.70 – £2.50 = £3.20$
Profit for 1 cup of orangeade:
$£3.20 ÷ 40 = 320p ÷ 40 = 8p$.
So each cup of orangeade sells for 12p + 8p = **20p**.

4) Cost of 25 candles from the factory:
$25 × £1.60 = £40$
Cost of 25 candles from the supermarket
(Raoul will need 5 packs of 5 candles):
$5 × £10 = £50$
10% of £50 = £50 ÷ 10 = £5
So after discount, the candles will cost
$£50 – £5 = £45$
The candles are cheaper at the **factory**, so Raoul should buy his candles from there.

5) Total area of lawn = 50 m × 40 m = 2000 m²
Amount mown in 1 hour = $\frac{250}{2000} = \frac{1}{8}$.
So if $\frac{1}{8}$ of the lawn takes 1 hour to mow, it will take
$1 × 8 = **8 hours**$ to mow the whole lawn.

6) If 6 red blocks make a tower 42 cm tall, then 1 red block is 42 ÷ 6 = **7 cm** tall.
Call the number of blue blocks b.
Then $(4 × 7) + 2b = 38$ cm
$28 + 2b = 38$ cm
$2b = 38 – 28 = 10$ cm (subtract 28 from both sides).
So 2 blue blocks are 10 cm tall,
which means 1 blue block is 10 ÷ 2 = **5 cm** tall.

7) Each day, the snail travels 2.5 – 0.5 = 2 m up the pylon, so it'll take 20 ÷ 2 = **10 days** to reach the top.

8) Fill in the information from the question first, then use it to work out the missing numbers:

	Castle	Museum	Total
Infants	15	5	20
Juniors	15	25	40
Total	30	30	60

9) Draw a quick sketch of the parallelogram (it won't be accurate as you only know one side):

12 cm

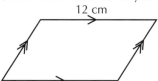

The perimeter is the length all the way round the outside of the shape. Parallelograms have two pairs of equal-length sides, so the bottom side of the shape will also be 12 cm.
The other two sides will be the same length as each other. Call the unknown length x.
So perimeter = 12 + x + 12 + x = 40
So $24 + 2x = 40$
Subtract 24 from both sides: $2x = 40 – 24 = 16$
Divide both sides by 2: $x = 16 ÷ 2 = 8$ cm.
So the other three sides of the parallelogram measure **8 cm**, **12 cm** and **8 cm**.

10) The first few terms of this sequence are
$(4 × 1) – 3 = 1$, $(4 × 2) – 3 = 5$,
$(4 × 3) – 3 = 9$, $(4 × 4) – 3 = 13$.
Johanna is **correct** as all these terms are positive and the numbers are increasing, so there will be no negative numbers in this sequence.

11) Manu is **correct** — one of the angles could be 90°, which would make the triangle right-angled.
Mike is also **correct** — one of the other angles could be 56°, or the other two angles could be $(180° – 56°) ÷ 2 = 62°$, which would make the triangle isosceles.
Owen is **incorrect** — all three angles in an equilateral triangle are 60°, so this triangle can't be equilateral.

12) Aalim's answer is **positive** as all square numbers are positive, then he's adding on a positive number, so the answer will always be positive.

Index

Index